'Brilliantly original, funny and insightful. Dry and comic, but also very moving. I absolutely loved it'   *Katy Brand*

'Gentle, heartbreaking, laugh-out-loud funny and poetically told – an intimate memoir that stays with you'

Rose Matafeo

'A deeply dark slice of comedic mastery'   *Sarah Solemani*

'A stunning book in which darkness and light, tragedy and humour, pain and hope are all masterfully, affectingly balanced'   *Liam Williams*

'Katy has one of the most singular and enviable minds working today (and tomorrow)'   *Jamie Demetriou*

'Brimming with graceful, charming writing – this book perfectly encapsulates so many moments we face as girls and women and I only wish I'd read it sooner'

Kiri Pritchard-McLean

'Fabulous story-telling and completely delicious writing'

Cariad Lloyd, host of Griefcast

'A layer cake of truth, pain and wisdom iced with charm. I loved it'   *Sue Perkins*

'Painfully raw and incredibly funny'   *Simon Amstell*

'Delicacy took my breath away'   *Lolly Adefope*

Katy Wix is a Welsh actor, writer and artist. She is best known for the TV shows *Stath Lets Flats*, *Taskmaster* and *Ghosts*. She has written two series of her own Radio 4 sitcom, *Bird Island*. She has written two acclaimed books of monologues for women. *Delicacy* is her first non-fiction book. She lives in London.

Katy Wix
DELICACY

A MEMOIR ABOUT
CAKE AND DEATH

HEADLINE

First published in 2021 by
HEADLINE PUBLISHING GROUP

First published in paperback in 2022 by
HEADLINE PUBLISHING GROUP

1

Cataloguing in Publication Data is available from the British Library

ISBN 978 1 4722 6120 5

Typeset in Scala by CC Book Production

Printed and bound in Great Britain by Clays Ltd, Elcograf S.p.A.

Headline's policy is to use papers that are natural, renewable and recyclable products
and made from wood grown in well-managed forests and other controlled sources.
The logging and manufacturing processes are expected to conform to
the environmental regulations of the country of origin.

HEADLINE PUBLISHING GROUP
An Hachette UK Company
Carmelite House
50 Victoria Embankment
London EC4Y 0DZ

www.headline.co.uk
www.hachette.co.uk

For D

CONTENTS

Introduction   1

1. The first cake   3

2. Anxiety cake   12

3. Jam roly-poly, or, Jenny nearly died
   in a car accident because her boyfriend was
   older and drove too fast   26

4. Lemon drizzle (for victims)   27

5. Muffin, or, Sat on a bench with a friend   50

6. Packet cake mix   51

7. Three-tiered Bundt cake, or, Idea for a sitcom   65

8. Low-fat cake, or, Being thin in
   capitalist spaces with your mum   66

9. Cigarette cake   78

10. Six cakes and six much smaller cakes   83

11. Doll cake, or, Three dolls I have met   106

12. Bara brith, or, Walking with my father   112

13. Mooncake, or, The disappointments
of fame   138

14. Oatcakes   140

15. Brownies, or, Oxygen mask   174

16. Birthday Cake, or, The most powerful force
in the universe   177

17. Chimney cake, or, The thoughts I have
about cancer when I open my fridge door
at night for a snack   180

18. Welsh cakes, or, Hand-written letter
to a best friend that I'll never send   216

19. Fruit cake, or, A joyless life   225

20. Welsh cakes 2, or, This page is about nans   227

21. Big pink cake, or, Dispatches from inside grief   230

Aftercake   268

Acknowledgements   277

Author's note   278

INTRODUCTION

The world is made of sugar and dirt.
— *Alfred Döblin*

What to expect from this book

These are stories from my life. Each story is named after a cake. The cake is in some way important to that story.

I started this book when I found my mind turning more and more to my own fragility. I felt deeply ashamed of this side of me and associated it with weakness, but knew I could no longer ignore it.

Many sensitive children work out that in order to function well in the world, they must repress their enormous capacity to feel, for fear of being 'too much' or, worse, abandoned.

Whilst writing this book, I often woke up gasping, having had the same dream that a stray dog had dropped a marble into my mouth, and it had rolled back to the opening of my throat. I can only assume that something had needed to be articulated, and words to be unstuck.

This might be a memoir about growing up in Wales, or it might be twenty-one things that happened to me, but the important thing was to excavate the emotional truth of it and, by writing, maybe lay it to rest.

Why cake?

Cakes are weird, camp objects that seem to appear whenever something emotionally devastating is happening to me. They represent everything that is false and cloying. I resent cakes: their condescending frilliness, the fact that they don't want me to tell the truth. When someone appeared with tea and cake in the middle of a family psychodrama, what they were really saying was: *Let's all eat our feelings instead of expressing them.*

Cakes are filled with trauma for me.

There has been a lot of cake in my life . . .

1.

THE FIRST CAKE

Our mothers always remain the strangest, craziest
people we've ever met.

— *Marguerite Duras*

Let me tell you why I rode my bike into oncoming traffic.

In 1992, shortly after I turned eleven, my family went on a family holiday, and I went with them.

'How far away from our house are we going and what sort of holiday will it be?' I asked Mum, the night before we left.

'Not far. And a cycling holiday,' she said.

'Can't we just walk everywhere?' I said.

'Why?'

'Just because.'

'You don't have to go fast,' she said.

'I never go fast,' I replied, and that was the end of the discussion. As she went back to struggling with the big suitcases, I could tell that she hadn't realised how much I really did hate cycling and being on bikes. I didn't even own a bike. When relatives said, 'How about we get you a bike this year?' I would say, 'Can I have something else?'

3

The plan was to spend a weekend bickering on the Channel Islands, before boarding a ferry that looked like a floating glass conservatory which would take us across the water, to the French town of Cherbourg. I knew the word 'Cherbourg' from the film *Les Parapluies de Cherbourg*, a musical where everyone sang an octave higher than necessary.

On our arrival in France, the man at the bike hire place said he had picked out a 'special bike for a pretty young girl', but the mocking of my adolescence in such a confident tone made me suspect he'd picked out one of the worst bikes from the pile. If this had been a film, it would have been the bit in a rom-com where the stable boy says to the protagonist from the city, 'You'll be riding Clover today, but don't worry: she doesn't go fast.' But it turns out that Clover does go really fast, and the fumbly city boy is teased for his inability to control Clover, and he looks stupid in front of his date, who is of course on a well-behaved horse and grew up riding horses anyway. At the end of the film they get married and the stable boy attends, doing a thumbs up in every photo.

I took my mum aside and said, in a stage whisper, 'Mum, have you forgotten that I failed my cycling proficiency test? Am I even legally allowed to ride this?'

'You'll enjoy it, once you're on it,' she said, smiling over at the bike hire man. 'It'll be good for you.' A violent phrase, if ever I heard one. When my mother was being playful, I wanted her to be more serious, and vice versa.

I had been the only child in primary school to have failed the cycling proficiency test. If I'd been allowed to walk next to the bike, and push it around the course, then I would have come top of the class. I was a good walker.

Oh great. I'm on a bike, I thought, as I got on. 'Fine. I'm on it. Where do I ride it?'

'On the streets.'

'What? Are you kidding?'

'Well, we're going to cycle into the town.'

'But there are so many cars.'

We set off, the whole family. I was already exhausted from a big dream I'd had the night before, and I kept having to pause every four minutes to adjust my lilac shorts and lower my centre of gravity, so that I would stay on. It was miserable. I could balance on it by now, but I couldn't take a hand off the handlebars without falling off. That's what the examiner had failed me on.

'That's it,' my mother called back over her shoulder. 'Just try and be steady, but also a bit loose.'

'I can't be steady and loose at the same – it sounds like you're describing hair gel, not a person,' I shouted back. It wasn't that I didn't enjoy the feeling of cycling – the freedom, the smells and sights of being outdoors – it was more that I felt unwilling to let myself be looked at whilst doing it, because I struggled to ride a bike, and I looked like someone who struggled to ride a bike, and I was so ashamed. The humiliation outweighed the joy.

As Dad overtook me he said, 'We can go to that place that does the nice ice cream for dinner tonight, if you like?' and instead of answering I rode my bike into oncoming traffic. There was no great mystery here: it was a protest against cycling, and a punishment to all who had allowed the cycling to happen. *This will show them*, I thought. I did try to warn them that I wasn't proficient. In that moment, I didn't care what happened to me, I just wanted revenge for being ignored.

I was fine. It had been a slow day, traffic-wise. One car narrowly missed me, slightly denting the basket, and the driver beeped and put his hand in the air. It didn't go down well. People were angry. I was delighted. My family and I walked back to the bike hire place in silence, just the squeak of the wheels and the growl of the odd car. The bike hire man saw the dent, refused to return my parents' deposit and didn't call me 'pretty young girl' again.

As we boarded the boat to take us back across the Channel, I said, 'I'm sorry about what happened with the bike.'

'Oh yes, that,' Mum said. 'But you didn't really mean to do it, did you, darling?' It was meant rhetorically, so I didn't answer.

It was time to go home. *I'll never ride a bike again*, I told myself.

The following year, my dad was working, so Mum and I went on holiday alone. We went to Paris for a few days, and this time the medium suitcase was enough.

'Oh, I thought you'd be a Chinese family,' the receptionist said as we checked in to our Paris hotel.

'Oh really?' my mother said.

'Yes, the "x" at the end of "Wix" makes it look Chinese.' He pushed the room key across the desk. My mum looked embarrassed, as if we had disappointed him, but I folded my arms to convey the comment's ignorance. The hand that pushed the room key was wearing a leather glove, but the other hand wasn't. Later, when he opened the door to our room, I saw that the hand in the leather glove was swollen.

It was a large tatty room, with two single beds and a TV on the wall in the corner. The cupboard doors didn't shut properly and one of the lamps didn't work. As I counted the dead flies on the windowsill, Mum unpacked a few things and it started to rain. 'Good for the garden,' Mum said, rubbing moisturiser into her neck in a sweeping upward motion. The plan was to set off early the following morning to find the house where my great-aunt had stayed as a student and, if there was time (there wasn't), to visit Monet's garden.

But later that night, as we lay in our single beds, to my horror, through the wall of our cheap room, we could hear sex noises. It was loud and mortifying, and just about the worst thing I could imagine happening to me at twelve in the same room as my mother. She didn't mention the noises, but to my relief turned the TV on to a news channel, to fill the room with something les vulgar.

The next morning at breakfast, she flicked a finger in the direction of a couple sat a few tables away. They were slab-faced and pink, like a pair of lungs.

'That's them,' she said.

'How do you know?' I asked.

'I recognise his cough . . . anyway, I think she might be an escort,' she continued.

'Why?' I said.

'No one can enjoy it that much.'

I sipped my grapefruit juice and watched the lungs throw sausages down their sunburnt necks. It looked like living.

My mother's hopes for me were that I would always be happy and thin. My hope for her was that she would never leave me.

After breakfast, we took a free map of the city from reception and set off.

'She was short, but she was beautiful, your great-aunt. A real head-turner, back in the day.'

We were standing on a street corner on the outskirts of Paris, looking up at the ornate brick building where my great-aunt had once lived during her training to be an opera singer.

'Did she have an amazing voice?' I asked.

'I never heard her sing, but she must have done. It was a good school.'

Pigeons sheltered from the rain in the alcoves of the windows on the upper floors.

'Was she famous?'

'No, she got married instead.'

Mum knew one story about my great-aunt. I'd heard it several times. Standing in front of her former dwelling, I asked to hear it again.

'Well,' Mum began, as two students emerged from the building carrying guitar cases, 'in her final year at the Academy of Music, she was so beautiful that when the examiner saw her, he instructed her to sing behind a screen, so that he could mark her fairly, without being distracted by her beauty.'

I thought about the cycling-proficiency examiner. When the test was over, everyone had gone up to the front of the class, one by one, and been given a certificate, but when I went up, I got a pencil. Now, I gazed up at a small window and imagined it was hers. I thought about how curious it was to be jealous of a dead woman.

We stood till it got cold, then found our way to a small café nearby. Sad French music played in the dusty tea room. The streets were quiet. The rain continued. Mum and I sat at one of the small round tables in the window. Mum asked the waitress to remove the glass ashtray. It was becoming the sort of trip that gave me a new appreciation for the comfort of my own bedroom, back home in the Vale of Glamorgan.

Then it happened. Mum went up to the counter, picked two cakes from the glass display cabinet and brought them over. Mine was cut into a perfect square, and arrived on a bright white plate. I took a bite. It had a sickly sweet smell and tasted like biscuits, cream and golden syrup. It was the best cake I've eaten, even to this day. A small squiggle had been iced on the top, the kind of design you might find around the door of a posh town house. I could tell, whatever it was, it was perfect.

After one bite, like an alcoholic taking their first sip, I knew I was in trouble. As the sugar hit and my eyes closed in ecstasy, I realised I had found my thing. Here was a cheap, easy and legal way of getting high, any time I wanted, for the rest of my life. What a relief to have found the answer so early in life: I would never be alone again, now I had discovered the magical effect of sugar. You're never really alone, if you're eating cake. Even later, when I chose cake over people, it felt lonely, but the cake lent such 'resonance to the loneliness' (as Marguerite Duras says of alcohol) that I didn't even mind or notice the loneliness. I never forgot my first cake, and I was destined to repeat the experience of that first bite, over and over again.

Whenever we sat in cafés or restaurants together, my mum's focus would be on intensely observing the people around us, rather than me. If she was close enough to eavesdrop, even better, and she was never happier than when she could make one of her pithy remarks, such as 'I think those two are on a date', or 'Oh, they must be having an affair', or 'I wonder how those lot all know each other? Teachers, I bet.' There was a table of teachers in every place we ever went, according to her. 'Curiosity is what keeps me young,' she once asserted. In this moment, she didn't even notice that her daughter was quietly becoming an addict. As I took the last few bites, my cheeks flushed and my throat was thick with chilled cream. I was suddenly very tired. My mother had only eaten half of hers and wrapped the rest in a napkin, slipping it into her handbag for later.

So we sat at our round table, with my empty plate where an ashtray once was, lost in our worlds. From time to time, we would turn back to one another, as if checking on a printer that you didn't believe would work, after pressing print.

But, when she turned to me, she must have missed the hum of the sugar working its way through my body. Even if she had noticed, there was nothing she could have done: I had tasted love. It was too late.

As we waited for the bill, Mum impatiently bobbed about in her seat, and I imagined that she was thinking about her childhood holidays in Wales, boating in Abersoch Bay. It was her favourite place on earth. 'Aber' means mouth of the river.

We walked back to the hotel. There was a small circular grid on the outside wall, which I hadn't noticed before. From the small hole, behind the grid, came the sound of violins. I looked through and saw that a string quartet was playing in the hotel foyer, just near to the reception, where the one-gloved man lived. Mum explained that they were local music students who were allowed to use the foyer to practise, so that guests could enjoy the music for free. The small hole afforded me such a perfect view of the musicians, but at the same time I doubted that was the purpose of the hole, just a nice coincidence. We stood for a while, in the breeze, enjoying the light coming through the iron bars, and just listened to the music, the taste of sweetness still in my mouth.

I have never eaten the cake since, or even found out what it was.

2

ANXIETY CAKE

People often ask me how I got into comedy.

Some of the men on the lawn were smoking. When they laughed they would slap each other's shoulders and their army buttons would bounce against their heavy, ironed uniforms. A large white marquee loomed behind them. Inside, their wives looked anxious and hungry as they arranged chairs in tight borders around dining tables before the guests arrived.

These army functions happened every year, in the height of summer. My whole family and I were expected to attend, because my English grandfather had been in the military all his life, and we were all scared of him. I was used to wearing black, but not black dresses that made me walk slower and showed off the tops of my boobs. The night before, I asked my mum to show me how to put on fake tan. She said, 'You mix it with moisturiser to make it look more natural.' I didn't, and now it looked as though diarrhoea was running down both calves.

As I neared the marquee, one of the laughing men peered out to look at me, trying to work out if I was old enough for him to fancy. I was tall for my age (and all ages) and kept needing to pull the dress down. A few weeks earlier, when I was getting out of the bath, my mum studied me, said, 'Welcome to puberty,' and shook my hand. I had cringed and closed the towel, but I understood what she meant. My body was different and no longer a neutral zone. Now, under the laughing man's gaze, I was excited to be a woman.

The intense heat gave guests the sheen of a Next catalogue. Everyone was old, and the women smiled into each other's bouffant hair when they hugged hello. I passed a ten-year-old boy in a suit jacket and kilt and gave him a look of consolation. When I saw other young people queuing up for orange juice, I held back with my empty glass so they wouldn't talk to me. It was simpler to stay with the adults, silently resenting them, and with no risk of peer rejection. A swing band was warming up in the corner, and the men's voices were punctuated by brass premonitions of the evening's music. The dance floor in the middle of the tent was empty, and bunting had been hung everywhere the wives could reach. These boring parties were some of the few times we crossed the River Severn, and in comparison to Wales the English countryside was more neat, the lambs more corporate.

Women stood by their men's sides, agreeing with things they said. This was casual misogyny in formal attire. Adults held wine glasses below their chins like microphones, as they watched a Major in a wheelchair struggle over the gravel. I had no respect for or interest in these adults, and the feeling was mutual. But my attendance implied I wanted to be there, and undermined my attempts to look bored.

When the gravel at the edge of the spacious garden was heard crunching under car wheels, men dropped their anecdotes mid-punchline, as heads turned to see who had arrived. Everyone was waiting for the royal car.

'Go and help your auntie in the kitchen,' my mother instructed, but, before I could complain, she was off, laughing by a fountain (a trait I didn't inherit).

I sulked across the lawn, towards the adjacent manor house. Older guests with large teeth stopped me to point out the resemblance I bore to my relatives. I said, 'Yeah, I know,' and they said, 'Round the eyes,' and I said, 'Yeah, I know,' again.

At the house, I opened the door to a factory of stressed waiters and caterers. I let in a wasp and the head defroster frowned and shooed us both away. A waiter close to my age, sweating in a branded waistcoat, passed me. We smiled at each other. He didn't notice my legs.

There were these women in my life. They were normal women, but I was encouraged to call them 'auntie' so they could demand extra cuddles from a child. They definitely weren't my real aunts: we didn't share blood, just wounds. 'Auntie' Yvonne was one of these women, and was now leaning over a large white cake at the back of the kitchen. She was head-to-toe in English florals, with one hairstyle at the back and a competing one at the front. Once a successful dancer and now not, she had danced and danced until she got hips and tits, they told her she was too big to dance and had to stop. She had delayed her 'Welcome to puberty' handshake until she was seventeen, by starving herself.

Without looking up she said, 'Oh, have you lost weight?' as if her ears were attuned to detecting people's fat store in their step. 'You know, there are a lot of very young handsome nice men here tonight,' she continued, spinning round. I shrugged. She handed me a piping bag, as if she were imparting classified information. She tucked my long hair behind my ears and said, 'You have such a pretty face, and you're tall. If you just lost weight, you'd look so striking.' I squeezed the piping bag until a blob came out.

Even by then, I knew the politics of being a tall woman. I grew up in a culture that wished all women would be shorter than all men. I knew that if you were tall, you had to be attractive. The worst thing you could be, as a woman, was tall and unattractive. A body that was both tall and un-attractive was a nightmarish object that would bring shame on the family, because it would be harder to attract a male. If you were a tall woman, then you had to either get really good at flirting or perfect that thing where you put all your weight on one hip to appear a bit shorter next to an insecure man, otherwise he would think that your body was trying to intimidate him.

Whenever Yvonne spoke to me, there was a feeling of being observed, but never seen. I was oddly mute around her. Perhaps it didn't feel safe to reply. Perhaps I didn't have the words to reply. Either way, I said nothing. I don't think Yvonne ever required a response: she just wanted to speak and hang up, like a prank caller. I got a lot of my early ideas about feminism from her: namely, act like it never happened.

The cake she had her face near to was square, with three tiers. Making cakes was how she held on to feeling like a good girl, and she made loads. She had created this one to be wheeled out at the evening's climax and, if necessary, eaten. It was covered in a generous layer of white royal icing. I've always hated royal icing: it's thick and looks fake, like the people at the party.

'Winter is your friend,' Yvonne had said to me once in the changing rooms in River Island, after another pair of jeans hadn't fitted me. I looked at the label and saw that she had given me a much smaller size to try on than the size I had asked for. 'Winter is your friend, because then you can cover up your body,' she said from the other side of the curtain, 'but I don't know what you'll do in the summer when you have to show it off.' Even now, as the seasons change, I still panic, and the sun brings with it shame and self-consciousness.

Back in the kitchen, a waiter with a tray of salmon canapés swung open the door to the garden. The band had started playing music that the guests would have danced to when they were young.

'Will you help me to ice on some English flowers?' Yvonne said, but then answered her own question with, 'I know: roses!'

She was a bad actress and I could tell that it was always going to be roses, and she knew that it was going to be roses before the men had even started putting up the marquee. Roses were the easiest flowers to execute in icing and Yvonne could take no risks: an ugly cake was a dereliction of duty.

She watched as I began piping the first rose on the top white square. From last year's do, I knew that the secret to good roses was to build them up slowly with layers of icing as thin as Rizla papers.

'Do you want the thorns part too, or just the rose part?'

'Don't be silly,' she snapped back, 'why would I want the thorns?'

She nabbed the piping bag and took over. She bashed out three yonic big ones. I left her to it. I was glad our blood was separate.

The party was in full swing as I walked towards the marquee. I noticed that the special royal guest had finally arrived. I looked at the wrong person, at first, thinking that they were the royal, because all the posh people looked so alike. It was only when I saw my English grandfather dive across the grass to shake the royal's hand that I realised which of the posh people it was. Despite my English grandfather's drunkenness, he spoke with a beaming confidence and didn't apologise for spitting. Royal aides stood nearby, giddy, watching over like proud dog owners. I didn't get spoken to.

As night descended, dinner began. I had to sit with officers, officers' wives and miscellaneous adults, at a round table smothered in bright linen. A waiter pulled out a chair for me as if I were someone old enough to vote. As I shuffled my chair in, he watched the way my tits moved, hefted into their new shape. Depending on the voyeur, sometimes my body was repellent and sometimes it was desired. I took these messages about my body very seriously, even then. If my body could have replied to these messages, it would have asked to be left alone and not judged. It just needed to be treated as some flesh that hung below me and be left in peace, whilst I got on with having fun. I felt sorry for my body: it was either always in or missing out on trouble.

The officer's wife to my right said that she enjoyed lifting weights on the weekend. Next to her was an elderly couple. The husband was so old, he looked like he could die from something as gentle as a massage. His wife bit her nails, which intrigued me. What have you got to be anxious about in your eighties? Next to her were Yvonne and her daughter. There was an enormous gap between their two chairs. And finally, another married pair. He was a big pillowy man with facial crumbs, bulked out by his wide, boxy jacket. His wife eyed the crumbs.

The table liked me: I was polite and quiet. I could adapt to whatever the adults needed me to be. At thirteen, you have to pretend to understand things even when you don't, or you might get laughed at. You don't own yourself when you are a child. A young person at the table serves the same purpose as a puppy or an iPhone. It is a distraction for, and bridge between, all the tense adults. Another fact of adulthood that bewildered me was the need to keep conversation shallow. Everyone always claims to hate small talk, but does nothing to stop it whilst it's going on.

The weight-lifter was kind, asking me what GCSEs I was going to choose. Her back stretched up towards the marquee roof, as if supported by celestial guy ropes. I had never seen anyone back home in South Wales with such good posture. I tried to picture what her bedroom would have been like as a young girl: the condition of her dolls and where they would've slept and whether they would have had their own doll-sized chairs to sit on. Every so often, the pillowy man stared at the weight-lifter's cleavage as though he was peckish, before turning back to his wife with a look of surprise (as if he had forgotten he had a wife) and annoyance (as if she had failed in her job to remind him).

The food arrived on large white plates. Everyone took a moment to survey the meal, admiring the careful arrangement of the chicken or fish, depending on which box they had ticked. Yvonne and her daughter sipped their white wine and looked around, ignoring the food. After the main course, they watched as the weight-lifter demonstrated some of her self-defence moves. *This is the first time they've seen a powerful woman*, I thought.

The pillowy man kept his eyes on the waitress's bum as she passed. The elderly woman grinned at me, before wistfully adding, 'Do you know what I miss? Smoking in bed and everyone knowing a poem by heart.' I nodded in agreement and thought about the young waiter that I smiled at earlier. I noticed that the pillowy man and his crumb-catching wife were quietly arguing across the table, maybe because he kept looking at the waitress's bum.

I couldn't tell if it was serious, or if they were just emotional and drunk.

The waitress returned with a bottle of red wine. As the pillowy man said, 'Thank you,' he reached out his hand and put his palm on the waitress's hip. He was looking the other way as he did it, so I couldn't tell if it was deliberate or not. His bored wife noticed his secret gesture and poured some water into his empty wine glass. She turned back to her fish.

After a few bites, she began to tell a story about once owning a florist's which had shut down. Before she got to the end, her pillowy husband interrupted: 'Small businesses like that always fail in Hampshire, that's the problem. It was doomed.'

'You're making me feel stupid now,' she said from behind her glass.

'It *was* stupid,' he slurred.

Everyone at the table cringed when he said this. I looked carefully for her reaction. She took a sip of drink, sighed, then stared off. Her dolls would have been arranged in order of beauty rather than brains, probably perched high on a wooden shelf out of reach, so they looked nice when other girls came to visit. Her father must have yelled and slammed doors or how else would she have ended up married to a pillowy man like this? He had already started a new anecdote, and was halfway through an impression of Neil Kinnock.

It was time for the cake. Yvonne was a bit pissed now and beckoned me with her towards the kitchen. She frantically searched for a cake trolley, spinning round the kitchen and giving me a view of both her front and back hairdos in quick succession, using flipbook technology to blur them both into one horrifying style. She placed the three tiers of cake on top of each other, holding them together by stabbing small wooden rods into each layer. We lifted it on to the trolley and stood back. It looked like the Bolshoi Theatre in Russia.

She was shaking with the excitement and the thrill of a busy day. I smiled at her, and meant it. I thought about the black-and-white photos I had once seen of her dancing as a girl, and how she had traded one regimented life for another. I didn't feel forgiveness towards her: I felt nothing, and that was progress. And I decided the front hairstyle suited her best.

I helped her push the cake across the lawn and into the marquee. Everyone clapped it, as if it had just sung a song. Yvonne cut the cake and I stood next to her, smiling with only my mouth, feeling too big and too small all at once.

When Yvonne and I returned to the table, everyone complimented her on the edible roses, and she fiddled with the delicate silver cross around her neck. The elderly man, who looked even older, tried to break the top layer of the rock-hard icing with his spoon. I sat down and thought, *This isn't a child's cake*, but it was sugar, so I ate it.

The pillowy man coughed like a gun going off and began to tell a joke. But people's attention was divided by Yvonne's tips on how to test if a cake is cooked, and so he added extra detail as he set the scene, trying to delay the joke proper until he had a full house.

Yvonne got the hint and shut it down. This was a joke with an important narrative build. I didn't want to listen to an adult's joke, but the table fell quiet, so I fell in line. Unsure if they should already be laughing, for fear of looking stupid, a few made little laughs, along the way, especially when he said the bit two-thirds in that went, 'So then the second bloke decides that he's going to try to get into heaven too, so he says, "Right, I need to do a good deed. I'm going to lend my wife my credit card."'

Then it happened. I realised that I knew this awful joke. I knew the set-up. I knew the narrative build. And, most importantly, I knew the ending. I'd heard it before on a TV programme late at night. As the joke began to descend, I looked around at the group.

Maybe one of them had heard it before too and they were just being polite? Maybe we all knew it? Perhaps it was a famous joke, which no one owned and anyone could tell? Excited by knowing it, I felt there was no way back. I could not escape what happened next. I felt compelled. I went for it, I said the punchline out loud.

The joke was over. Everyone had heard me say it, but no one laughed. There was a long pause. The pillowy man, without engaging other muscles apart from his neck, turned to face me. He was red and silent. He didn't look me in the eye. Both fists were clenched tightly and his head was red and vibrating. I smiled until he looked down at his sugar rose.

Respect and shame flashed across his wife's face, perhaps even the hint of a smile.

She's glad it happened, I thought, *she loved it*.

I was giddy as I understood what I'd done and the humiliation of the pillowy man. I wondered if his wife was feeling what I was feeling and pictured her leaving him. Her leaving note would say, 'Dear Pillowy John. I hate you almost as much as I hated that joke. Love, your wife.' Maybe I had helped in some small way.

He didn't look at me again for the rest of the dinner. Yvonne stared at her daughter and she looked like she was going to cry. The pillowy man hummed with anger as he wiped cake crumbs from his mouth. Drunk with power, I sat back in my chair and chewed with my mouth open.

I left the table to go to the toilet. There was another lawn in the grounds, connected to this lawn by a narrow path, at the bottom of which was a row of luxury Portaloos. The toilet signs were two Victorian figures: a man in a top hat and cane, and a woman with a parasol, who looked coyly over her shoulder, back at the viewer, as if to say no one ever shits in here.

Leaving the faux-Victorian cubicle, a divorced woman at the bottom of the steps asked if I had a lighter. I washed my hands and left. Beyond the loos was a strip of gravel on which stood the waiter with the nice smile, smoking a cigarette. He was looking straight at me from within a haze of smoke, so I walked nearer to him and then turned my body side on, because I thought it was my best angle. It worked, because he said something like, 'Hey,' and then I said, 'Are you working here tonight?' and then he said, 'Yeah.'

He offered me the cigarette, but it wasn't a normal cigarette. Why did all the naughty boys have such nice smiles? I took a drag and handed it straight back. I hoped that he wasn't going to ask for my name: I didn't like saying it out loud. I had only just started speech therapy to cure my lisp, and I didn't like saying my name yet. I imagined him taking my hand. I would be nervous and wouldn't know what to do, so he would part my lips with his own, to ease me in, which is what kissing is, I imagined. The divorced woman asked for his lighter, then said, 'Do you think my hair looks dyed?' and tried to put on his waistcoat. I left them to it.

I walked back across the dark, empty lawn. The marquee loomed on the horizon like Snowdon. The muffled music was punctuated by roars of laughter. The evening was still warm. As I approached the narrow path, a shadow appeared up ahead. Walking unsteadily towards me was a person. As they got closer, I realised it was the pillowy man from dinner. I tried to move past him, but he blocked my way. Faced with his overwhelming masculine energy, I wished I was back in my normal baggy clothes and Dr Martens, so I could run away. My silly heels began to sink into the grass. I couldn't meet his gaze, but I could tell that he was angry. He stood with his feet spread apart, either for balance or for authority, and stuck out his palm as if instructing a dog to 'stay'. When he used my name, it was the same feeling as when a personalised ad on the internet addresses me by my name: invasive and manipulative.

I looked around for help but knew there wasn't any. I could hear my own heartbeat. His eyes were dancing with anger. I wanted to cry. My dress may have been grown-up, but my pants were pastel pink with 'Saturday' embroidered on them. I didn't know what he wanted and it was scary. Neither of us spoke.

There was something in his eyes besides rage. Did he want to slap me? Was he turned on? Would he devour me like one of the canapés? The job of the bully is to kill the child within themselves, so that they will never have to feel small again, and will never have to confront their own fear of vulnerability. Ruining his punchline had unleashed a weapon and I was braced for his counter-attack.

He pushed his hips forward and opened his mouth.

'Listen to me, young lady, never EVER interrupt your elders when they are telling a joke.'

I had forced this man's anger to the surface. I had power. Here was a man with over fifty years to get a joke right and I could already do it better at thirteen.

He stopped swaying for a moment and we stood still, letting the insects bite us, just the sound of his breathing. I wanted to run, but my dress was too tight, so I walked as quickly as I could, back towards the lights and faint sounds of the party. It was exhilarating.

And that's how I got into comedy.

3

JAM ROLY-POLY,
OR,
JENNY NEARLY DIED IN A CAR ACCIDENT
BECAUSE HER BOYFRIEND WAS OLDER
AND DROVE TOO FAST

Jenny pretended her jam roly-poly was curtsying, by holding out the plate it was presented on and dipping it. Our Home Economics teacher applauded. Jenny dipped the plate again. The rest of us clapped too, but we didn't know why. It was like a moment of mass hysteria – if we didn't clap, then something terrible would happen, like we would all start crying.

4

LEMON DRIZZLE (FOR VICTIMS)

The basic recipe

Crack the eggs into a bowl

I met Jodie one summer evening, by the stone wall, outside the only three shops for miles around. She was sat smoking, in the dark, with two other girls from the village, their cigarettes glowing like the electric bars on my nan's old heater. I was with a girl called Ceri. She was quiet, like me, but she was just quiet, whereas I had a feeling like I'd been born with someone else's silence that was never really intended for me. I was on the brink of turning into someone. I was waiting to meet the right person, who would unlock this upgraded louder personality. After fourteen years I had carried it to term, and now it was ready to be born. I was impatient to change.

This was the stone wall that always had teenagers puking or falling over near it. Though I'd never hung out there, I was aware of its reputation. There was no rule to say that anyone couldn't go and lean against the wall after dark, but we were still making a plucky move. When Ceri and I would pass the wall at night, the light of the one street lamp would fall on the girls' faces, illuminating their big hoops and painted features. We wouldn't pause: we would slow down our walks as we passed and maybe force a casual 'Hi' if there was any alcohol in our bloodstreams. Even though Jodie and her gang were only a year older than me (I was fourteen, to their fifteen), they had the allure of having lived longer.

We hadn't planned to go over to the wall, it just sort of happened. Maybe it was the new moon, or the need for a new thrill to talk about for the rest of the summer holiday.

Ceri and I stood shyly, a few metres away from the girls. From afar, Jodie's eyes looked huge, but up close I could see this was just the effect of layers of black liquid eyeliner. When she drew on her cigarette it looked like she was slightly smiling, but I think it was a dislike for smoking that she was trying to hide. She didn't say 'Hi' back when we said 'Hi', even though her two friends did. Jodie's power, I decided that night, lay in not giving a shit – a non-attachment to people and events which both impressed and scared me, like Eckhart Tolle. *Even the adults can sense this*, I thought, as I observed them, avoiding walking their dogs near the wall at night. Ceri stood a little too close to me. I studied Jodie's body for clues on whether she was bigger or smaller than me, under her baggy clothes, and wondered who had taught her to use hairspray like that. It can't have been her mum:

I'd seen her mum, and she had no style at all, choosing to dress in a way that could only be described as 'vulnerable and sporty'.

'Sit down if you want,' Jodie grunted. I nodded and said my name, even though she hadn't asked. The effect of being next to Jodie was immediate: two boys soon wandered over, tall and gangly, arms and legs out of balance with their small, spotty heads. I recognised the taller one with the shaved head. Everyone fancied him, but I didn't know his name. He passed around a small bottle of whisky and we all took sips and then laughed for no reason, with our hands in our pockets, looking down at our shoes when we spoke to each other. When Jodie talked to the boys, she expertly stuck her hip out; it wasn't my hip, but it might as well have been. That hip spoke for all of us. We wanted the boys there. Jodie put in a fresh chewing gum, gestured towards the taller boy and whispered in my ear, 'That's Huw.' I fancied him, so thank God I was wearing my favourite jumper (which was fake Benetton from Cardiff market, but passed as real every time). Later, Jodie said, 'He wants to get off with you.' But I didn't let him.

Ceri said that she was tired and wanted to go, so I gave her my house key. A few nights previously, Ceri and I had turned up late to her house to find her massively Mormon father hand-painting quotes from the Mormon Bible all over the kitchen cupboards, whilst her mother slept upstairs in their indigo bedroom. In the low kitchen light, we could see the wet, black paint still shining: 'The fear of the Lord is the beginning of knowledge,' it said, just behind her father's head, on the plate cupboard. I wanted to stay there, intrigued to see her mother's reaction, but Ceri was freaked out, so we left and walked silently to mine.

She had been sleeping on a camp bed on my bedroom floor for the past two nights. Ceri's dad was the first person I had ever seen to lick his thumb and forefinger and then put out a candle. I must have been very young, because it made me gasp. Or maybe I had gasped because Ceri had cried, hurt that her father had been too impatient to let her try again to blow out all the candles on her birthday cake. Her father's justification for this had been that girls didn't have the same lung capacity as boys. Somehow, I had the courage to stand on my chair and shout, 'Sexist pig.' I was only about eight, but I felt that her father and I had got the measure of each other that afternoon.

Two nights later, I stayed out till nearly midnight with Jodie, just wasting time, walking around the village, telling stories, and talking about which bit of the village we were going to walk to next. She said that we would hang out again another night and that Huw really liked me, but he was really popular with all the girls.

That night, once everyone was in bed, I got out my diary and wrote, 'I think Huw and I are soulmates, but once we've kissed, I'll have to move aside for the next girl.' I went to sleep hoping that my boobs would be a cup size bigger and my hair an inch longer by morning. I wanted life to hurry up.

The following weekend, I babysat for a family who lived in the nicest part of the village. I stood at the foot of the twins' beds, waiting for them to tell me where the key to the Welsh dresser was. They asked:

'Why?'

'Because that's where your dad keeps the dictionary and I need it.'

'For what?'

'I'm doing an essay.'

'What's it about?'

'You're too young to understand.'

The truth was, the dresser was where their dad kept the video cassettes. In amongst Mr Powell's fishing videos, I had spied a copy of the 1979 erotic historical drama *Caligula*, famous for its supposed un-simulated sex scenes. I decided that as soon as their parents left, I would put the children, whom I regularly babysat, to bed early, and watch the film and think about Huw. I wondered if it was possible to become good at sex just by watching it done, rather than actually doing it. Without access to the internet, the closest I had come to seeing a penis was being able to spot Orion's belt, on a clear night. But the key was nowhere to be found, so I had to make do with Mrs Powell's copy of *Memoirs of a Geisha*. Around midnight, I was woken by the sound of Mrs Powell's heels in the hallway. 'Oh,' she said kindly when she saw the open book lying next to me, and recognised the blanket wrapped around me as being the one from her bed. Usually, when I was alone in their house, babysitting, I acted with great embarrassment, as if there were cameras on me or something, but on this night, for some reason, I had done this. She put the book (also taken from her bedroom) on the coffee table, folded the blanket and gave me the cash. She didn't seem to mind. She had an expensive haircut and long earrings that made her look like an anthropology lecturer, but I didn't know what she did with her days. I liked her though. She seemed different. She had the air of someone who was doing whatever she had originally planned to do in life, which was refreshing. Whenever I babysat for Mrs Powell, just as she was getting ready to leave she would always tell the twins to be good for me, then she would tear up as she said goodbye to them, even though she would be back in a few hours. And she always came back early anyway, like a loyal family pet. She was my dream person to babysit for. She seemed easy to talk to, which was comfort enough at that age, without having to actually talk to her. I also liked her because she had named her beagle after an obscure Egyptian mother goddess, 'Ipy', plus she was often ill, which made her highly relatable.

When Mrs Powell dropped me off at mine, I stood outside the front door for a moment, looking at the empty street, enjoying the aloneness. Then I wondered how girls are supposed to relate to their bodies, when no one else is around. I noticed Mum peering out of the top bedroom window, looking for me. I hadn't been alone.

As soon as the whole house was asleep, I phoned Ceri to tell her that I hadn't watched *Caligula* or found anything sexy in the opening chapter of *Memoirs of a Geisha* (which was written by a white American dude, anyway), and that I thought I was probably going to kiss Huw soon. She said that she'd had a masturbation breakthrough: 'If you do it with a Yellow Pages placed on top of your stomach, then it feels better – like the weight of another person.'

One Saturday, several weeks later, Jodie and I spent the afternoon in her plush bedroom, half watching *Robin Hood: Prince of Thieves*, but we kept having to pause it to talk about ourselves. She downed some Fanta and began a long story about the time she was a bridesmaid, as I plaited her long, lovely ponytail without being asked. If she went wrong, she would start the story almost from the very beginning, but I didn't mind. I was the listener. Ceri was my listener. It's OK to be the listener as long as someone listens to the listener occasionally.

Jodie always wanted to come to my house, which was frustrating, because I always wanted to go to hers. My father didn't like having visitors much and her bedroom was bigger. Jodie had been allowed to swap her normal lightbulb for a red one. She kept cider in something called 'a keg', in the corner of her room, and a 'Do Not Disturb' sign, in red letters, hung on the door handle outside, the type you find in hotels. Co-ordinated wallpaper and roller blinds too, in gold-and-cream horizontal stripes, which had the effect of feeling as though I was in the bedroom of a celebrity's daughter. All allowed by her father, because he was off work, with stress, and this stress spurred him into giving his children whatever they wanted.

Her house was in the posh bit of the village, not far from the Powells. I was intimidated by this part of the village, it was all big lawns, white cars and jeans. We had a garden, but it was 50 per cent paved. Her mum called us into the dining room for dinner. Their dining-room table looked as though it was floating, because it had a glass top, and when we all sat down I could still see her whole family's bodies through it, and my own. It was disconcerting.

When Jodie announced she was going to the toilet, I died because I hated having to endure a second of interaction with her family without her there, especially now we were all adjacent in a glass display case. When Jodie left the room, we all waited in silence for a few moments, then her mother untucked her necklace and said, 'Would you like a drink?'

'Just some tap water, please,' I said. She cantered out to get the water filter jug. I hadn't seen one before, so I just stared, not sure what to do. 'Please tell me your mother doesn't give you tap water,' she said with a laugh, pouring water into my frosted glass, thrusting her chin out, affording me a sudden flash of an uneven septum. 'I don't know,' I lied and looked down the carpeted corridor towards the bathroom. Even the tops of their doorways were arched. All our door knobs were loose.

The first time Jodie stayed at mine, at breakfast time she swallowed a whole spoonful of Vegemite, thinking it was chocolate spread, then spent the next half an hour trying to smell her own mouth. Next time we were in the supermarket, I brought this up to try and persuade my mum to buy Nutella.

Once her parents were in bed, we made obscene phone calls, by picking random numbers from the Yellow Pages, then breathing and moaning before giggling and hanging up. When it was really dark, the two lads from the stone wall appeared by the back door, can in each hand. We let them in and we all stood looking at each other, with sudden adult expressions on our faces. We moved, quietly and in sync, like a quartet, to Jodie's big bedroom. Huw and I sat on the floor, Jodie and the other boy sat on the bed, the thick plait hung down her back and they giggled, ignoring us. Huw and I barely knew each other outside of this room, but it didn't feel that way. I asked him if he had a dog and he said no. He showed me his key chain and I said, 'Cool.' I hoped I looked pretty in the electric red of the bulb. We talked and drank for ages, edging closer to each other on the rug, until we were kissing.

He pulled away and said, 'You have eyes like Kate Winslet.' 'Thanks,' I said. He put his hand on the back of my neck, and guided my head towards his middle. I took his hand off from my neck, but he did it again. I didn't want to put him in my mouth. The excitement of the kiss had come and gone, now I just wanted to leave, but felt stuck. The bed seemed like an altar from my position, down on the rug. The two of them were also kissing. I saw the boy touch her through her clothes. He put his hand on her boob, but only for a few seconds, like he was testing the temperature of the tit, but didn't touch the other one. From below, it looked like he didn't make contact.

'Are you going to take your jeans off then?' Huw said to me in a hushed voice. I didn't want to be left out, or for Jodie to think I was a baby, so I did. I took them off. A few minutes later, there was the sound of footsteps suddenly and all four of us did our best to look innocent, with such short notice. When her father opened the door, I realised that the Do Not Disturb sign was just for show. I hadn't had time to put my jeans on all the way. He didn't say anything. He slowly put his hands in his pockets. After a brief pause, he told the boys it was time to leave.

Then it was just the two of us again. I climbed on to the bed with Jodie and said, 'Did you do it?'

'No.'

'Did you?'

'No . . . but like almost.'

'Really?'

'I let him touch me and stuff.'

'Oh my God, you did that in my room? That's gross.'

'Oh . . . sorry . . . I . . .'

Then she laughed, so I laughed too. She tickled me under my chin, but then pulled the skin, quite hard. 'Ow,' I said, getting off the bed again. 'Sorry,' she said, still laughing, 'it's just something I do with my brother, it's a joke.' But her face, even through loads of make-up, seemed more babyish somehow. I wondered if the kids who became sexual soonest did so because they looked older, or if it was the other way round.

At least something had happened to me. At least I was living.

The summer was over. I didn't see her again for several months.

Beat together 225g softened unsalted butter

Of all the goddesses, Athena is the one I relate to the most. If I had to choose a temple to visit right now, or a cult to join, it would be hers. Because, firstly, in some versions of the story, she was Zeus's first thought. She was born from an idea. My mother had the idea that she was lonely and needed something to love, so she had me. Secondly, my worst creative ideas take months to develop, whereas my best ideas seem to arrive fully formed, as Athena did from Zeus's brow (and in full armour, ready to fight).

Whenever I feel stressed, or tired or silenced, I hide out in ideas. That was how I coped with being bullied – I tried to think about it conceptually, rather than how painful it was, and thought I could distract myself from the experience by sleeping loads, or focusing on schoolwork, but it was hard to concentrate.

I loved English lessons, but I don't think the teacher thought I was particularly smart. If she did, she never let it show in her words or face. She didn't want to be a teacher any more, anyway. She was just doing it until she and her husband had enough money to open an Italian restaurant in Cardiff Bay.

The boys who sat behind me liked to talk about fingering. I would forget to tune them out during the lesson. I think I mainly heard them. It didn't matter anyway, because intelligence and looking as though you were trying were things to be embarrassed about at my school.

One day, out of the blue, one of the boys was expelled and I didn't know why. The rumour was that he had taken a rabbit from the woods, at the edge of the school, gone to the boys' loos and drowned it. You can be prosecuted for drowning a mammal, even a mouse. It was a few days after this event that Jodie joined the school, as if it had been a straight swap – one in, one out – but I knew it was just coincidence. I wondered how she instinctively knew how to be popular and if it was because she acted as though she was already popular. What intrigued me more was how she had worked this out on her own. Where was she getting this great knowledge from? She looked the opposite of nervous. New kids were usually given a hard time, especially considering that she had come from a private school (where the girls wore burgundy hats at a jaunty angle) to our comprehensive. 'Her dad literally had a breakdown, we should be nice to her,' I heard a girl say, when Jodie walked into the English class. When she didn't sit next to me, I thought, *That's OK, she's her own person.* The lesson was on *Pride and Prejudice*, which I found boring. I found plot boring. I think I still do – well, maybe not boring, just a little needy. I discovered that I enjoyed poetry a lot more than novels. The outdated school library had a small poetry section: both the Thomases, R. S. and Dylan, Blake, Milton, a couple of war poets and then something odd like a copy of the poems of Clive James.

We had a lesson on Elizabeth Bennet's character, and the teacher asked the class to get into pairs and then decide what we thought the most defining moment for Elizabeth's character was. When it was time for me and a girl called Iola to report back, I said, 'Is it that Elizabeth Bennet is defined by what she doesn't do, and the decisions she doesn't make – she's held back by the traditions and morals of society around her.' The teacher shook her head and said, 'Characters are only revealed through what they do, not through what they don't do.' The next person said, 'The bits with Darcy,' and the teacher said, 'Correct.' When I handed in my essay she just wrote 'No' across it in green pen.

When someone doesn't think you're smart, it's easy to believe that you don't have anything to say or write about, and even if you did, no one would be interested in hearing it. But, equally, have you met people who have been told all their life that they can do anything? – They're awful.

The next lesson was art, my favourite, but when I got there no one would sit near me. I didn't understand at first, but when it happened again the next day and in every lesson for the rest of the week, I realised that it was because of Jodie. She had spread a rumour that I had stolen an eyeshadow set from her and that I'd had sex in her bedroom. I sat at the big table in the classroom on my own, with an anatomy book in front of me, drawing this big skull, which weirdly looked like my mum's friend Jean. 'Anatomy is important if you want your drawings to look alive,' the teacher continued. Jodie whispered to some of the other girls, then they would turn to look at me. Finally, the art teacher got up and sat next to me. She stank of coffee. It was the single most humiliating moment of my life.

The next few weeks were horrible and confusing as I

became more and more picked on and isolated. After a few weeks of this, I decided that, in order to survive, I needed to make a new group of friends, to end the long, lonely lunchtimes. I made friends with a girl who was partially sighted. She showed me where she would hang out at lunchtime, with the other shy girls, behind the library. I didn't really like any of these new girls – in fact, I secretly thought that I was funnier and smarter than them, but at least I was adapting and surviving. One of them had come to school that day with a metal tray down her front, under her jumper, because another girl had threatened to punch her in the stomach if she came in. She had to stay standing all day because of the tray.

I went round to the partially sighted girl's house for a sleepover and fake-laughed my way through dinner. Her dad could tell that I was faking and eyed me with suspicion. I think he knew that I didn't really get on with his daughter. She was very nice, there was just no connection.

I pushed a boy with a shaved head like a kiwi fruit into a locker as hard as I could, then denied it to the teacher, as the boy stood there crying. Victims can be violent people too.

Just the sound of Jodie's name began to frighten me and I even dreamt about her. When the alarm went off in the mornings, I would lie there, not wanting to get out of bed, and then at the last minute I would get up. Every time she would call me fat or weird or stupid, I would pretend that I hadn't heard or noticed. The most important thing to me was that people didn't see that I was being bullied. Optics were everything. When I sat in the loo, hiding, eating my lunch, I recalled something I'd read in a book in the school library about how the wives of disgraced samurais might also decide to commit suicide, along with their husbands, but before killing themselves some would tie their knees together, to prevent the shame of their legs falling open, even after death.

Once it became more violent, then I had to respond. She cornered me in a toilet one day and said my hair looked greasy, insulted my mum, and put out her hand towards my face, but slowly, like we were underwater. I didn't wait to find out if her intention was to harm me or not, quickly lifting my hand to protect myself. As I did this I accidentally scratched her face with my locker key. Things escalated after that. We had arranged to meet in the local park, one night after school, for a fight: her gang against my gang (Ceri and me). I didn't want to go through with it. I was scared, of course, but the shame of not turning up was greater than the fear of going. I don't know what I was expecting to happen, but I took a golfing umbrella with me as a weapon, the type that had a large metal spike on the end. When Ceri and I got there, she was standing in the middle of the park with three other girls. She had on cherry-red Dr Martens with steel toecaps (her weapon). There was a bit of kicking, shoving and pulling of clothes, then suddenly Mrs Powell was running towards us from the other side of the park, her beagle trotting behind. She was out of breath, telling us to stop. We had. Jodie spat on the ground just in front of me and said, 'You're not worth it anyway,' and walked away. Mrs Powell, Ceri and I stood there. 'What's the story here?'

Mrs Powell finally said, which almost made me giggle. It was a strange way of phrasing the question. I never found out, but I think she must have told my mum what had happened, who then went into the school. Things got better after that. Jodie and I didn't speak to each other again though. But I was left alone.

As much as I hated being bullied, it sort of sharpened my focus, in the way that being lost in a new place does. It made me hyper-vigilant. Or maybe it's that the shame was so great that it filled me up, right to the top, and gave me a sort of purpose. Being a victim was a full-time job. In the way that being really into a conspiracy theory might be easier than accepting chaos. As the psychoanalyst Stephen Grosz puts it, 'Paranoid fantasies are disturbing, but they are a defence. They protect us from a more disastrous emotional state – namely, the feeling that no one is concerned about us, that no one cares.'

There was a strange intimacy between Jodie and me, knowing that she was out there, in her bedroom, plotting against me.

The real shame was not that it happened, but that I couldn't stand up for myself. I worried that maybe it was my fault. That maybe I hadn't been a good friend and I didn't know how to be a good friend. I knew it wasn't me, but, also, it was me. It wasn't my fault, but I was the one it had happened to. How did she sense that I would be so bully-able? Nothing like that has ever happened to me since, but I do make myself smaller around other women occasionally, because of the experience: worried that if I get too big, share a success, I'll cause someone to be threatened, and it will incur their anger, and I'll be punished and betrayed again.

Add the finely grated zest of one lemon

Mrs Powell said that when you are ill, you can't imagine being well again, which is the same as saying when you are enemies with someone, you can't imagine ever being friends.

In 2006, I was sitting in my space (my bedroom), when I got the message on Myspace. I didn't recognise the name straight away, because she was using her married name. The message simply said:

I'm sorry I was a bitch. Can you forgive me?

She was shorter and kinder-looking in the photo than I had remembered. I had always pictured her still living in the same village, or at least one nearby, not exactly being happy, but being popular still. The party days were over and she was a changed woman – at least, that's what the two small dogs she was cuddling in the photo seemed to be saying.

Numbness and shock were my first reactions. I stared at the screen, not knowing what I should do or feel. I suppose some sort of instinctual obedience must have kicked in, like I was begrudgingly writing Christmas cards, because I began to type:

'Of course, I forgive you. It was years ago now. We were only young, we're very different people now. We were teenagers. Let's just move on . . .'

As I was writing it, I thought things like, *This is so kind of me* and, *This is the right thing to do* and, *It feels good to do the right thing* and, *How nice of her.*

I'm not sure why, but I didn't press 'send'.

A few days later, I recounted the whole thing to my therapist during our session and told her what my draft reply had said, waiting at home to be sent. She said, 'And is that how you feel?' and I thought for a while, and then I said, 'No. No, that's definitely not how I feel,' and she said, 'Well, don't send it then,' and I thought, *What a good therapist.* So, that evening, I replied with the truth instead. 'No, I don't forgive you,' I wrote and pressed 'send'.

It felt like the sort of event that would end up in a book, years later.

A few moments after that, I was sat at my laptop, but now in the crash position and worrying if I had done the right thing. I decided to write down my feelings in my feelings journal that my therapist had told me to get:

I don't even know what forgiveness really means anyway. Does it have to be said out loud or written down or what? Is it synonymous with forgetting? To forgive, you forget, is that it? It could be more the absence of emotion than an emotion itself, no, perhaps it means being able to speak to that person in the future without being passive-aggressive – that's what forgiveness looks like, in a real sense. Is forgiveness even an emotion? You can't just say you forgive someone and skip over the anger stage. You've got to get angry first, even if it takes ten years or more. The Myspace message

KATY WIX

has just reminded me to be more angry about it. I feel worse. Rejecting an apology is actually very difficult. I remember my English grandfather once saying something like, 'Women are just more forgiving by nature.' It had never occurred to me until this moment that forgiveness might be gendered in some way. Did my gender mean that it was expected that I would be more forgiving? I worry that I relish her suffering. I worry that, if I forgave her, then I would no longer have the excuse to be angry, to be depressed or to act a certain way. I would lose my victim status, which affords me self-righteousness, tea and sympathy. And so I worry that forgiving will diffuse the energy I get from running away from my victimhood. I could suddenly wake up one day and throw my whole career away, realising that it's been built on this need to prove my worth to this group of kids that were mean to me one summer. Killing my story, the one I've had for years, would mean letting go of the joy of suffering. And suffering as protest. It would minimise what happened, let her off the hook, give her what she needed. It would make her Christmas nicer. It would mean having to forgive myself for not standing up for myself. It would mean forgiving myself for behaving like a victim. It would be admitting that people aren't one thing and can slowly change. It would mean admitting that we were alike and that I can be horrible too. It would mean not enjoying the fact that she would be waiting for an answer. It would mean letting go of the idea of some future revenge. It would mean coming out of the crash position, into a more relaxed stance. It would mean seeing her as a person, rather than

45

a villain. If I was secretly planning on never forgiving her, then this will mean changing my plans.

She might not have changed. This might be a test. Once I send it, that's it – can't bring it up again, or ask for another apology. I'm more excited by the version where I don't apologise – what would happen next? I wait for her to reply, and we keep on corresponding about how sorry she is, and how I don't accept her apology, for the rest of our lives? I don't want to die with regrets, but I think I already will, so whatever.

But if I don't forgive her, then nothing changes.

I stay the same, and so does she.

Sift in 225g self-raising flour

I ate a vegetarian breakfast in the B&B and waited for the car to arrive. This was in a remote part of Scotland. I was now thirty-five. The driver, a bespectacled man in his late forties/early fifties, waved at me from the driver's seat and I got in. He was nice and friendly.

About ten minutes into the journey, I noticed that he was grinning at me in the mirror. And I thought maybe it was a nerves thing. But he looked almost proud, sort of misty-eyed. It made me slightly uncomfortable. The more he smiled, the more I didn't want to. Something about his intention made me want to look away. We were quite close to where he was going to drop me off for the filming. I don't remember what the film was. When we were close to the film set, he said, 'You went to school with my wife.'

And I knew what was coming next, I just knew.

The next morning, when he picked me up, he walked around and opened the door. I was a little late on account of the deep breathing I needed to do in my room before leaving, to try and keep calm, knowing he would bring it up again. I apologised, smiled and got in the back. As we made our way through the country lanes, the same thing began to happen – the smiling in the mirror, but this time it was more a smile of pity. On the passenger seat beside him, there was some cake in a Tupperware box. After a while he said, 'Jodie is doing comedy now too.'

'Oh right,' I said, not caring and, frankly, deeply suspicious.

'Yeah, well, she's written some stand-up comedy,' he added.

'Oh right,' I said, wishing he would stop.

'She wondered if you would read it . . .'

And I wanted to say, 'Are you fucking kidding? Of course I don't want to read it,' or something like that, but instead I said, 'Oh . . . yeah, I'd love to, but it's probably better to see it performed and I've actually got a bit of a headache, sorry . . .' and put in my headphones.

I wanted someone else to read it and tell me what it was about because I was still intrigued. I started to wonder what he knew and why he didn't look ashamed. Maybe she had told him a different version of events, or maybe he didn't know about the Myspace message. But he kept looking and looking at me, like he had decided that he was going to reunite us. When we got stuck behind a flock of sheep, he opened the Tupperware box and took a few bites of what smelt like a lemony cake.

'That looks good,' I said. I was never not nice, I just didn't show that anything was wrong, the same as I didn't back then.

'It's home-made,' he said.

I bet she made it, I thought. He held out the box, offering it to me. I shook my head. *Obviously, I couldn't eat a cake she had made*, I thought. *It wouldn't just be a cake any more, then the cake would be an idea, and the idea would be forgiveness.*

He ate it loudly, as the sheep stumbled around the car. He must have been fourteen, fifteen years older than her.

Then he said, 'Yeah, she couldn't believe it when I said that I was going to be picking you up. Such a weird coincidence, isn't it?' I stared out of the window. Whenever he started talking about it, I just felt so ashamed and angry that he knew this secret thing about me, especially when I had worked so hard to be someone else now. Also, he spoke as if we had some sort of relationship, and we didn't. We were strangers. He just seemed so desperate to fix the situation. And then he said, 'She might be staying in your B&B tonight, actually.' I started to play out all the different ways in which we might bump into each other when I got back there, later that evening. What would I do or say? At least I knew that I could stand up for myself now.

Beat together with 225g caster sugar until pale and creamy

The next day, I was sat in my trailer, on the film set, when there was a knock on the door. I opened it, and a runner told me that someone had turned up on set, saying that they knew me and that they wanted to say hello. I didn't really hear all the words properly, in my panic. 'Can you say I'm busy?' I told the runner. Then I hid in the toilet, long enough, I thought, for the visitor to get bored and leave. I never found out if it had been her, but I can't think who else it would have been.

As I sat in the small toilet cubicle, with my head resting against the plastic wall, other small details about her life started to come back to me. I suddenly recalled her wiping away tears with the sleeve of her (real) Benetton jumper on non-uniform day. This was after we were no longer friends. I remember her rushing out midway through a maths lesson and afterwards hearing the maths teacher say to another teacher that it was 'a difficult time for her family'. I had completely forgotten about passing her house and barely recognising her thin, gaunt mum, mowing the front lawn.

When I think of her now I still don't feel forgiveness, but I feel closer to her. I remember the things that drew me to her in the first place, but not enough to want to bite into the enemy's cake.

5

MUFFIN,
OR,
SAT ON A BENCH WITH A FRIEND

The pigeons want our muffin crumbs. Their eyes continuously moving, beaks open.

This bench is almost equidistant from where we both live, but my journey is slightly longer. She throws the rest of her muffin on the floor, exasperated.

The pigeons seize it, their boat-shaped bodies all around our feet.

Finally, my friend wants to talk.

'I really do love my girlfriend, but she didn't even notice when I dyed my hair pink, the fucking bitch.'

6

PACKET CAKE MIX

> If dieting is the answer then what is the question?
> – *Susie Orbach*

When my boyfriend came out, it wasn't a huge shock because a big part of our relationship had been talking about fabrics.

We met during the summer holidays, working at a puppet festival. He wasn't one of the puppets, he was a real boy. Making puppets was how he sometimes earned money. I was in charge of ticket distribution, so sat in a wooden hut all day with no computer: everything was handwritten. The first thing he said to me was, 'Wow, that's so pink,' because I had persuaded my mum to sew a fuchsia faux-fur collar on to a leatherette jacket from Peacocks, to make it more unique, and it had caught the puppet-maker's eye. We bonded because we were both about to turn twenty. On the last night of the two-week-long puppet festival, we kissed beside a burning barrel. He had an older sister who worked there too, who had a much older Marxist puppeteer boyfriend. When his sister saw us kissing she looked pissed off.

She didn't like me because I made her puppeteer boyfriend laugh and she couldn't. Plus, I predicted everybody's choice correctly when we sat around the burning barrel on the last night, guessing everyone's favourite song. I was incredibly good at the game and was briefly popular as a result; it was a shame that I only got popular on the last night. But then I got too confident and joked that I was going to burn all the puppets on the fire when everyone was asleep, and not one person smiled or laughed. The older Marxist puppeteer's favourite song was 'Writing to Reach You' by Travis.

We dated for a few months, but it was the sort of relationship where we talked on the phone for an hour, once a week when we were a bit drunk or after his late shift at Harry Ramsden's. Apart from fabrics, we didn't really talk about anything of substance. He said he was scared of being a waiter all his life, but other than that I don't remember finding out much about who he really was, apart from the anal porn stuff and that his parents were really supportive of him. We only met up once. He picked me up from Swansea train station in his mum's car one evening. When he turned the engine on, a song from the musical *Jesus Christ Superstar* came on, loudly, making me jump, and he said the CD belonged to his mum and quickly turned it off. He lived with his parents in a static caravan in a big residential park. We walked past rows and rows of neat small bungalows, some perched atop red-brick bases, like cars in a mechanic's garage. As we approached his front door, with the bin bags and dream catchers outside, I thought I'd better start acting more like a girlfriend: mature, big-eyed and ethereal. I offered to take off my shoes and he did a small incredulous laugh at the idea that someone wouldn't. His parents were in the front room, on large light-grey sofas, watching *Crimewatch* and eating ice cream from bowls. The room glittered with mirrors, twinkly mermaid figurines with colourful glass bodies and hanging crystals. A small dog was curled up asleep on a plastic garden chair, by the big window. We politely said hello to each other, and I told his mum that we had the same bowls in our house, only in blue, but then he pulled the sleeve of my jacket, so we quickly headed to his tiny bedroom. We burst in, all giggly, and shut the door behind us. I saw two texts from my mum to check I had arrived safely, but ignored them. We lay on his bed, looking up at the ceiling, and laughed nervously at nothing in particular. He slagged off his parents and I asked a lot of follow-up questions, pleased that I had stumbled upon a subject that energised him. The sounds of *Crimewatch*, and spoons scraping against Argos porcelain, seemed so close by in the compact house. I glanced at the side of his face and saw that he had one speck of glitter on his prominent cheekbone. There was a sudden knot in my stomach as we leant in to kiss, because I remembered how we had bashed teeth when we kissed the first time, but this kiss was better. We were more relaxed. I hadn't eaten all day because I was too excited about seeing him in the flesh. The night before, I'd gone to sleep with my (brand-new) mobile phone on vibrate, resting on my stomach, so that his texts would wake me. I was obsessed with him, but obsessed with everything anyway, at that age, so it wasn't necessarily significant.

He accidentally trapped my hair under his elbow, so I helpfully sat up to scoop my hair out of his way and drape it over my shoulder. That's when I caught a glimpse of the porn mags, anal and heterosexual, just sticking out from under his bed. I wondered if there was more under there and if it was all anally themed, all heterosexual, or if that's just what happened to be visible – the tip of the anal iceberg. As it got dark, he grabbed a tall bong from his windowsill, full of old bong water, and we set off to the nearby Spar mini-supermarket to get some cheap cider. 'It's OK, I don't smoke, like, all the time, you know,' he said as we left the micro-store and walked to a dark corner of the nearby park, holding hands. We passed a few other young people that he nodded and said hi to, mainly boys in dark tracksuits and polo shirts. Once we were sufficiently wasted, I sat on his lap on a stone tomb in the graveyard. His fingertips and lips felt cold. 'You said on the phone you were going to get condoms for tonight,' I said after a few moments. 'Oh, sorry, I forgot,' he said innocently, but I went a bit red and felt oddly rejected as I freed myself from his grip to bend down and tie my shoelace. 'What's the matter?' he said. 'Nothing,' I said and shrugged. I pulled a stupid face, puffing out my cheeks, to try and be funny and ease any tension. He didn't laugh and said, 'Be careful – people will beat you up round here, for being weird like that.'

When we got back to his static home, his mum had left out cheese sandwiches and crisps for us. We ate them, our eyes so red in the bright kitchen lights. I looked to see if the glitter had gone from his cheekbone, but mainly I tried to remember who he was and why I had even liked him in the first place. I decided that I was smarter than him, which was good, as it meant less pressure to be pretty. It didn't matter if I looked disgusting as I devoured the food (something I often believed must be the case when eating in front of boys). Usually I liked guys who were smarter than me (or who I perceived to be smarter than me). But, with him, I could mention any book I'd ever read and he would say, 'God, you're so smart,' and I would like that more than any compliment he would give me about my appearance. He suggested watching a film, which I was delighted about because I was too warm and fuzzy and full of white bread to be seductive now. 'It's cool that your sister goes out with an older guy,' I observed, looking at the family photos on top of the telly. He looked almost confused for a moment, and I thought I'd said the wrong thing. But then he said, 'He's only thirty-two. That's not that old.' 'Oh, yeah, OK,' I said, agreeing immediately. 'It's not like he's fifty or anything, like my stepdad.'

We heard voices. A couple had stopped beside the static home. They were arguing about something that had happened in the pub they'd just left. We placed sofa cushions under our knees, so we could peek out of the window at them. We mimicked their drunk voices and arm movements. The pissed couple were either too drunk to notice us or weren't interested in us. We threw a bit of bread at them, then snapped the window shut quickly. We laughed and it was the laugh of certainty that only the young can really afford. The laugh of people at the idea that they would ever let themselves get that old, or pot-bellied, sunburnt, or bald or bitter or unhappy, or chaotic or disappointed. He looked like his mum when he laughed.

As one gets older, one continues to laugh at the idea, but only with less and less certainty. Before we realise it, we're closer to the pissed middle-aged couple than the twenty-year-old mocking them from the window.

When I was on the train home the next morning, we texted the funniest direct quotes from the drunk couple that we could remember. It wasn't as funny the next day, and I felt like absolute shit, but I was overjoyed to have so many new private jokes with him. It was a love language. Having private jokes with someone is as serious as getting engaged.

Three days later, I sat bolt upright in bed, the phone buzzing away on my stomach, but it was a text from someone else. Another three days passed and I still hadn't heard from him. I rang his mobile, no answer. I rang his landline and his mum answered and told me that she hadn't seen him, but that she had seen Catherine Zeta-Jones's mum 'out and about posing' in Swansea city centre. I left a message for him to ring me back, but he didn't. I refused to lose my dignity and ring again.

I would put my aching heart into the bath and cry and wonder what I had done wrong. It had been a month now. Why did it hurt so much? Everything felt more dramatic in the bath. I thought about turning to religion or jogging, I felt so sad. It was like a deep, deep hunger that couldn't be sated until I had heard from him. It was like the pang people get to be near the sea after they've moved away from it.

One evening, when Dad was at work, and Mum was out at the supermarket, I went into the kitchen and looked through the cupboards for anything sweet. The best time for bingeing was just before Mum did a big food shop, because items would be quickly replaced and were therefore less likely to be missed. No one would notice that I had eaten forbidden foods. Because I was encouraged to diet from a very young age, and Mum hardly ate, there were always two types of food in our house: women's food (Ryvita, low-fat cottage cheese, apples and skimmed milk) and men's food (everything else). At the back of the tea and coffee cupboard was a packet of instant cake mix, one week out of date. The type that you only have to add egg and water to. I sat alone in front of the TV, in the comfiest armchair where Dad usually sat, with one piece of the cake on a plate, still warm from the oven. I didn't bother to make the icing. There wasn't time. Mum would be home soon. When I'd eaten that piece, I returned to the kitchen to cut another slice, until it was all mouthfuls and mouthfuls of chemicals, fat and butter, and I'd eaten the whole family-sized cake. Right after the binge was the part I hated the most. I couldn't escape my body. That was when the self-hatred and shame and disgust were at their most piercingly painful. I suddenly reflected on this middle-aged couple that I'd seen on a TV show once. It was a husband and wife who said that they had been driving through the French countryside, and that they had got lost and it was getting dark. Realising that they weren't going to find their chalet in time, they turned down a country lane, following a big red sign, next to a bridge that said 'Motel'. The woman said that, when they went inside the motel, they were greeted by an old man with white hair, a long plum-coloured shirt and brown trousers. He couldn't understand them, even when they spoke in French, which they attributed to their terrible French. They ate a meal of thick, sweetened bread and cheese, in the empty restaurant. The pictures on the walls were all of swans and they looked, somehow, three-dimensional. The old woman who owned the hotel was wearing a long white dress and white apron, and carried a small dog. The husband interjected then and said, 'We just thought it must be what they wear in rural France, you know, and we sniggered a bit.' They both agreed that when they were shown to their room, the beds were very high, with a bolster on the feather mattress. There was no glass in the windows, just wooden shutters, and the door closed with just a latch, no lock, so they put a chair up against it. The next morning, after a good night's sleep, they went back down to reception and were only charged nineteen francs. The couple both agreed that they were shocked at how cheap it was, and that had included the meal too. Before the couple got back in their Vauxhall Astra, the husband decided to take a photo of his wife, stood outside the motel, next to the overflowing hanging baskets. At the end of their holiday, as they made their way back down the motorway, they passed the same bridge, the same red sign for the motel, and they decided to pull off, once more, down the small track. They drove up and down the small lane several times, but the motel had disappeared and the trees that lined the road, which had been short, were now very tall.

Two weeks later, they got their photos developed, but there was one photo missing – the photo of the woman outside the motel.

The couple were on TV because they claimed that this was evidence of time travel and that they had gone back in time. It was a very serious programme. It didn't seem to be mocking them. Food was my way of controlling time. Not eating was a way of attempting time travel. Every time I refused food, I was investing in my future self, a better me. Conversely, every time I binged, I was fixed on the past, because bingeing is always a message from a past self about trauma. Not eating is a rebellion against a grown-up body and a grown-up world. If binge-eating could speak, it wouldn't have a future tense.

Forbidden foods must be eaten quickly and in secret. Bingeing wasn't about pleasure or being in the present moment, it was an act of aggression against myself. And bingeing would quickly be followed by purging. By the age of twenty, I was already in the grip of this cycle of starving and bingeing and self-loathing. When I wasn't thinking about what future foods I would eat during my next binge, I would be thinking about all the past foods I had missed when I was hungry. If the goal of eating too much was to be pleasantly numb, then the goal of not eating enough was to be alert, anxious and disciplined. I was in pain.

The idea of travelling through time is so hard to resist.

*   *   *

When Mum came back from the shops, I held my distended belly, but wouldn't say what was wrong. I watched as she began to put away the shopping. Soon she would start cooking dinner and I wondered how I would fit in any more food and what I would say. Whilst she boiled the water for the pasta, I looked to see which customary diet magazine she had bought this time. I pushed aside some carrots on the work surface, so I could open up the magazine and marvel at the stories inside. This could be my story too. The women inside were posing in bikinis in their thin 'after' photos. They had finally figured out how to never obey their appetites and to always remain hungry, and had, at last, become lovable and fuckable. I would read the details over again, memorising how they did it. Love was possible. Someone would meet my outrageous needs if I could just memorise a few weight-loss tips. Without the magazines there, to remind me that I should constantly be trying to improve myself and my body, then I would descend into chaos, happiness even. 'Your body is a job,' the magazines would wail as a chorus, and it was a life-long job. You must never have a day when you are not trying to be smaller, tighter, toned, younger, prettier, fresher, natural, hairless, more approachable, accessorised correctly and lovable. Diets are a time for absolutes: thin or fat, good or bad. Sometimes the hunger would keep me awake at night. I would distract myself rather than feed myself. Feed others, not yourself. Some experiences just aren't for me. Eating is a spectator sport.

If only I'd known then what I know now: that nothing

triggers chaotic eating like a diet. According to Susie Orbach in her seminal book *Fat Is A Feminist Issue*, over 90 per cent of diets will inevitably fail, trapping the dieter in a profitable cycle of failure and resubscription.

I took a few bites of the spaghetti Bolognese Mum had made. I'd filled my stomach like someone might overfill a room, so you couldn't even open the door. I had failed. Young women were supposed to be desired and pretty, not moon-faced and depressed, pretend-eating pasta with their mums. I looked at her and wondered when and how I had somehow got the message that, despite knowing that I was smart, my real goal should be to have someone fall in love with me; that would be the pinnacle of being a girl.

'Do you remember those cakes we ate in Paris, Mum?' I asked.

I don't know why I had thought of it. I sometimes had daydreams about going back, retracing those original steps and trying to find that dessert again, the one I had loved so much. Perhaps the café no longer exists. Even if I were to find it and eat it again, I don't know what I think would happen. Even if it did taste amazing, I doubt the thrill would even last till evening. Or maybe I would find the place and burn it down.

'No, darling. I don't.'

The next day, I was doing squats in the garden as punishment for eating the packet cake mix, when Mum shouted from the living room that there was a phone call for me. I recognised his voice straight away on the other end when I said hello, and thought that maybe he had been crying. He said that he had been on a train to Cardiff with two of the puppets he had made, when he fell asleep, and someone stole them from the overhead bit. He was almost yelling at me, as if I had done it, even though he was just trying to recreate the anger. He wasn't angry at me. He paused to catch his breath. 'Were they in a bag or anything?' I asked.

'Why?' he said curtly.

'I just wondered if they knew what they were stealing or if it was like . . . a surprise, when they looked in the bag, after they'd taken it.'

'Well . . . they were in a blue duffle bag, so maybe a surprise, I don't know. I just can't believe no one said anything or stopped them.'

There was a silence. 'I often put my leg through the strap of a bag, and put it on the floor, if I think I'm going to fall asleep, and I'm on my own . . .' Another silence. 'Did you tell the police?'

'Yeah, when I got off the train, I told two policemen at the train station.'

'Will you get them back?'

'Well, they couldn't say for sure . . . Anyway,' he concluded, 'thanks, I actually feel better now, I thought I was going to have a total meltdown about an hour ago, but I'm OK now.'

'You haven't been in touch in weeks,' I blurted out. I could see my reflection in the living-room window, still sweaty from the squats. I could see how I lowered my head as I said this sentence, in what I've come to realise is my 'telling men the truth' pose.

'What? That's not true,' he protested.

'No, it's been weeks,' I repeated. There was a brief crackle sound on the line. 'Hello?' I said, sounding worried.

'Yeah, hello. I'm still here ... I wanted to call, but I couldn't think of what to say.'

'OK,' I said quietly. The crackle was there again. 'Why are you calling now then?'

'Because I was upset ... and because the puppet thing reminded me of you, I suppose.'

'Oh,' I said, curling the telephone wire in my fingers. I watched Mum begin to hang out washing in the garden. I said that I should go. But then he said that the other reason he was calling was to say that he'd realised that he was into guys but not to tell anyone. I nodded on the other end of the phone, but was quiet and Mum smiled at me through the window. When he said, 'But let's just be friends though, yeah?' I knew that I didn't need any more friends, as mine were all perfect. I was full. We ended the conversation with me telling him that I was proud of him and that I was sorry about his puppets and that I definitely wouldn't tell anyone, and I meant all of it. He tried to make a joke that was from the store of our private jokes, but I didn't find it funny any more.

As soon as I hung up I realised that I was relieved that I didn't have to have sex with him now. I wouldn't have to worry about taking my clothes off in front of him in his cold room, whilst still holding my body at attractive angles. And

I wondered if I had known he was somehow unavailable all along, and if that's what I had secretly wanted, because it was safer and easier. Now that he was gone, I could get back to my real life: the fantasy of finding happiness. And I thought about the middle-aged couple who'd claimed to have time-travelled. Their story could be seen as being more about their fear of other nations, and their interpersonal problems, than anything else. Maybe time travel was easier to grapple with than dealing with a relationship. Also, at no point in the story did the motel owners (supposedly from the past) express alarm at the sight of a Vauxhall Astra.

Years later, maybe five years later, I saw him pissed in a supermarket on his own, holding a basket full of bacon. He kept telling me I looked beautiful, 'like a beautiful doll' he kept saying. 'You always looked like a doll to me.'

7

THREE-TIERED BUNDT CAKE,
OR,
IDEA FOR A SITCOM

A divorced nutritionist misses his wife and children so desperately that he disguises himself as three-tiered Bundt cake, leaving himself on their doorstep. The family bring the cake inside and the nutritionist is thrilled to be back in his old home and near to his loved ones again. The man's ex-wife and three kids are all taken in by the deception, leading to much poignancy when the nutritionist hears himself discussed in (what appears to be) his absence. Six half-hour episodes.

8

LOW-FAT CAKE,
OR,
BEING THIN IN CAPITALIST SPACES
WITH YOUR MUM

Nothing aches like a heart.
          – *Gemma Collins*

You are eleven years old playing in your room when you hear your mum shout from downstairs, 'Do you want to go to a disco?' You do. Put on your best party dress and red velvet hat. Wait impatiently by the front door calling for her, as she pins up the sides of her hair and hunts for the car keys. Drive twenty minutes out of the village towards the big roundabout. Mum parks the car, saying, 'OK , we're here.' But when you look up, out of the window, you realise that she must've said 'Tesco' not 'a disco'. Remove your hat out of embarrassment. She smiles at you, stifling a giggle. Later that night, when you overhear your mum relay the incident to your dad, when they think you can't hear, they will laugh and your dad will say that he'll tell that story on your wedding day, one day. (He won't.)

Despite the humiliating start, you still have to help Mum do the weekly big shop. You drag your heels a few steps behind her. As a child, you always felt tired the moment you had to do something you didn't want to. Supermarket shopping makes you feel tired.

You've been coming to this big Tesco, near the round-about, for years. When you were tiny, you were treated like food: placed inside the trolley amongst all the shopping, and you would try to stand up as Mum pushed you round. You would try to clutch her hair with your small hands each time she bent down to place something in the trolley.

Once inside the store, the bright lights make you squint and the sound of feet squeaking on the shiny floor reminds you of how big school sounded, when you visited, ahead of starting next autumn. Any item not on the shopping list will need to be pitched for if you really want it. Despite your pleas by holding the items (body spray and Pop-Tarts) up to her face, the answer will always be no. Stick to the list. She is too beautiful to disobey, anyway.

You keep up a bored expression as she goes on about saving money, and how foods with longer shelf lives are usually placed towards the back of the shelf, so you have to stretch your whole arm to get them. You ask if you can get your nose pierced. 'And what if it gets infected?' she says. You ask if you can go vegetarian. 'If you start emptying the bin in your room, and only once you've stopped growing, then maybe,' she says. You ask if you have a short neck and she says, 'Your hair's so long at the moment, it's like a cloak – maybe it's making your neck seem shorter?'

You listen to her voice go much higher when saying hello to a tall woman she secretly doesn't like, by the peanut butters. You feel embarrassed when they stop for a chat and block the aisle with their trolleys at an awkward angle, so that people have to move their trolleys around them. Cringe when the tall woman says, 'Ooh, hasn't she grown?' to which your mum replies, 'Yes . . . she's going through the braces and glasses phase at the moment,' and you smile politely, revealing your braces even more, which feels cruel. When there is a lull in their conversation, the tall woman looms over you and says, 'And how's school, hmmm?' and you suspect she is the Grand High Witch, from *The Witches*. You stand close to your mum and pretend not to hear the question. 'Oh, didn't you know? It burnt down,' Mum says, with excellent comic timing, twisting an earring back into place. And the tall lady looks at you with her mouth open, wanting more details, but you don't say anything because you don't like speaking outside of your home yet. So you don't tell the tall woman how you watched your small village primary school burn from your bedroom window one night, dressing gown tied tight, your groin pressed against the radiator for comfort. How you wondered if it was your artwork you could smell burning, or the plasticine melting. How you heard your friend's older sister say that the boys who broke in and did it were 'rough as fuck'. How you had to have all your lessons in a church hall from then on. And how strangers donated new stationery and Rich Tea biscuits.

*   *   *

Food shopping after big school is tiring. Big school is exhausting enough. The only thing you like about going to the Tesco's is that it's full of strangers. You enjoy the mystery of strangers. Until you know someone, they are enigmatic and captivating. You stare at shoppers' faces as they pass you. You are trying to work out how the world works. Now you are a teenager, you spend more time away from your mum and the trolley because you want to assert your independence. You offer to fetch things on the other side of the store for her. But really this is so you can flirt. The supermarket is a great place to practise wanting. You tie your school jumper tightly around your waist, so your tits stick out more. You walk past a shelf displaying lubes, on your way to the bread aisle, and act like you know what they are.

You pass a boy you like the look of, from the back, then spin around to see his face, front on, when you get to the end of the aisle, so that your long, dark (cloak of) hair will stream around you. You see a really fit boy in the cereal aisle. Unexpectedly catch sight of him again near the frozen ready-meals, and perhaps even risk eye contact. You continue to play peekaboo with him till you see him again at the checkout, when you get nervous and look away.

You try to work out what makes you attractive to these boys, the differences between your body and theirs. Sometimes the dads notice you too and you can smell their armpits on a hot day, when they stand too close behind you in the checkout queue.

Your mum's high blonde hair will make it easy for you to see her quickly, when looking down an aisle of shoppers.

You always spot her first, but then she will look up, as if she knew you were there, or maybe she just acted like people were always looking at her. In less busy aisles like 'World Foods', you might suddenly find yourselves alone for a moment, and you quickly check your face in the small make-up mirror that always lives in your mum's handbag.

You stare at your mum, as she chats with the lady on the checkout. Feel grateful to be loved so much, by anyone, let alone someone like her, who is so expert in loving – despite the fact that you suspect she was badly loved herself. She strokes your arm, but you don't respond and unload the shopping on to the conveyer belt as it moves forward. You take care not to let the young cool couple behind you see what you are buying because you don't want them to know personal information about you and a weekly shop is way too revealing. You don't like the idea of this couple seeing your salad cream, your tampons or your first deodorant. This is because you are a Pisces, but also because people knowing what you desire is embarrassing. You recall those TV shows where the presenter shows a family what they eat in a week, by displaying it all on a trestle table in their backyard, like a puppy having its nose rubbed in its own shit. You wonder if shaming people into changing ever works.

You watch Mum search for coupons in her handbag. You recall all the nice things she has done on previous trips, like give money to the homeless man who sits outside the store entrance and help elderly people with their bags.

Think about how weepy she gets sometimes, like when she is sat on the end of her bed, crying because she can't fit into any of her thin clothes. You stand patiently in the doorway of her room just listening, hoping that she will see what you see. Years later, think about how you mother your own body.

When the checkout woman asks how many bags you want, you successfully predict how many you'll need. It's always seven. You picture your nan, shopping and cooking with her mother and she with her mother. You will be tempted to feel guilty, in a few years, when you are the first person from your family to go to university, but try not to.

Mum says to wait there whilst she gets the car. You find room on the bench outside the store and steady the brimming trolley in front of you, with one hand. The homeless man isn't there, you notice the absence of his smell. You don't mean that as a judgement, it's just a very specific smell which is part petrol, part something you can't identify.

You wait for Mum's car to appear. You study your thighs. Panic because you can't remember what the car looks like. You wait a bit more. You remind yourself that a large part of being young is waiting. Wonder if children experience time differently to adults. Your motto will one day be: *One of the greatest pleasures in life is things being over*. Realise you don't have your mother's thighs. They are more like your dad's; thin, with long femurs, so easier to break. You know this because your dad broke his thigh bone when he fell off a stage once. Painful as it looked, it meant that he couldn't work and had to be at home with you. You loved it and enjoyed cutting up his steaks and taking them up to his bedroom.

You get older. On results day, you will ask your university tutor if you got a first and when they say no, think, *Well, it was still worth it because I made a lot of friends*. But you do wish you'd read more. You never fully know what you are studying towards and don't trust your brain anyway. You wish you'd eaten more. You consumed only bananas, gin and small amounts of pasta with tomato sauce from a jar, the whole three years you were there. You are happy with a 2:1. You wonder how you're going to become a famous performance artist in the next six months. You'll think television is too mainstream for you and can't imagine ever wanting to perform on television. In your third year, you'll take part in several experimental live art pieces. Join a small performance art collective. Feel euphoric whilst performing. It all goes well until someone tries to cut their body, on stage, as part of their art, and the whole thing is shut down.

A boy in your hall of residence says to you one day, 'You're a lot more serious now you're thin,' and you'll say, 'I know,' apologetically. But it feels more important to be thin than funny right now. You learn the phrase 'diametrically opposed' and use it in all your essays. You have fun. You forget whose elbow that is touching yours when you wake in the mornings, and whose bed it is. You watch your friends drink bottles of water on dance floors at 2 a.m. You try to dress like a girl called Nancy who always looks incredible and applies lip balm a lot.

After you graduate, you'll move back home and your mum will still drag you out of bed in your skunk-scented room, at 9 a.m. on a Saturday to go to Tesco with her.

So there you are, your mum and you going up and down the same aisles, in the same order, just as you always have, except now you are twenty-one.

You notice how ugly the place is. You didn't see it before. You notice the women's toilets has a new mural of a dandelion on one wall, which makes it look like it is growing out of a sanitary bin. The café is now a pale apple green, like a children's hospital. The neon lights are the same, the servers look younger, the recycled air tastes the same, rowing couples, dead flies, stale scones – all the same.

You notice how Mum is dressed for the supermarket as if she were going into town. There is something glamorous about her that some of the other mothers didn't have – you didn't see that before either. She wears bright, bold printed dresses that she has probably sewn herself, gold dangly earrings, and her hair is home-dyed. She tries to teach you how to sew, over the years, but you'll think it too gendered and too technical. Following a pattern is hard. You're scared of following all her patterns. You don't like the sewing dummy that she keeps in the corner of her bedroom, because it's headless and creepy and smells of lavender.

Standing by some mushrooms one day, you feel your whole body clench with sadness as you realise that you'll never make your mum happy, but that it's not your responsibility, anyway. The night before, she drank too much white wine and said, 'I could've been ... so many things ...' on her way to bed.

She gives and gives to others, cares for others, and doesn't expect the same in return. You realise that you are probably trying to fulfil your parents' unrealised creative dreams, and yet she demonstrates to you that womanhood equals martyrdom. It's confusing.

Others won't see her sadness, because she'll put on a show. They'll see only her charisma and self-assurance. Her longing will be subtly stitched into her lining, for only you to glimpse.

Now that your body has got used to hunger, you are thin. Women will show more interest in what you're buying. Now you are thin, you enjoy putting unhealthy foods in the trolley, to show the world that you are not obsessed or starving, but that you are just normal, healthy and happy. In the same way that there is that trend of very thin actresses posing in pictures with junk food it was hard to believe they had actually eaten.

You're tired. 'We're almost done,' Mum says. At the end of the bread aisle, there is a woman handing out free samples of cake. 'Oh what a treat,' Mum says, popping the sample bite in her mouth. 'Who doesn't like cake?' the woman beams back. The cakes come in a pink box. The packaging is confusing and patronising. No surprise, I suppose – products marketed at women are often quite patronising. It's also like they are selling sex. The cake is about temptation, naughtiness and desire. The cakes also come in a special low-fat diet version, which is in a lighter-pink box, to suggest less vibrancy. The special diet cakes taste like biting into air. Above the picture of the cake on the diet version there is a sort of halo, indicating controlled desire. This cake represents the cake you are not eating, the pleasure you are not taking, the life you are not living. All cakes should come in a plain brown box, like cigarettes, but marked 'Cake', and maybe what type of cake, but that's it.

The shopping is done and everything has been stuffed away into the boot. You sit in the car and Mum pulls the diet cakes out of their light-pink box. The cake is broken into four pieces and placed on a tissue that she balances in her open hand. It is all so peaceful and cosy, except that you don't want to exist.

You are thin. But you feel cheated and as though you have been lied to. You aren't any happier. In fact you hate yourself more because now you are so empty and tired. You don't have the energy for romance, you don't feel small enough anyway despite what friends say, and the hunger keeps you adrenalised and awake at night. Being thin means nothing. Your internal experience of who you are hasn't changed. The women's mags told you the problem lay within you, not the world, that it wasn't society that needed to change, it was you. They promised you a day when you would finally get the love you wanted and deserved if you could reach your goal weight. It's as if you have finished a game of pass-the-parcel that lasted for years, only to find no gift at the centre.

A smaller body has little to do with intimacy, joy, pleasure, connection and power. All thinness gives you is a feeling of having a body that doesn't stand out.

You don't trust the diet cake. Your taste buds still remember proper cake. You look out of the window at the sad, abandoned trolleys. You both stare ahead at the back of the supermarket building at whatever ad campaign they are running. Mum complains that the women in the photos, all around the building, are all under thirty-five, which doesn't accurately reflect the true age of the average woman that shops there. You aren't listening.

'What's wrong?' your mother asks you, noticing that you are distracted.

There is a panicked feeling in your stomach and then you gradually speak: 'I don't know . . . I'm not really interested in life.'

She frowns, studying the cake in her lap.

The sentence feels much worse to say than you imagined.

Dying was a fantasy, really. You just wanted certain parts of yourself to die. The important thing is – you have said it.

All those years you spent together, shopping for food, even though you complained, a part of you loved the relief of feeling mothered. For a moment, you could stop having to be a tough teenager, putting all that exhausting energy into image management and pretending to be harder than you were, more confident and more rebellious than you were.

Being in Tesco with her, just for those few hours, meant being in no rush to grow up.

Years later, your mum tells you that the reason why those boys had broken into the school was because they were hungry. They had tried to cook food in the kitchen and had accidentally started the fire. You feel relief.

9

CIGARETTE CAKE

I got back to my student halls, and my first love had stuck a note to the door. It said that his nan was ill and that he'd gone to see her, and that he'd be back in two days. I called him, with the tiny bit of reception I was able to get in my dorm room, but he didn't answer. I had an essay on *Medea* to write, so I lay on my bed with my books. His nan must've become ill suddenly, because he'd never mentioned her being unwell before. He'd never actually mentioned having a nan before, but then we had only known each for three months. Besides, at twenty years old, having a nan is something that you assume about each other, without having to go into details, like having a Young Person's Railcard.

The essay topic, if I recall correctly, was along the lines of monstrous or perverse portrayals of motherhood and female self-destruction. I just had time to write down the sentence 'The worst thing a woman can do is . . .', when my friend texted me about meeting her for a drink, and she wouldn't take no for an answer.

On my way to the pub, in-between wondering if *Medea* is ever taught in female prisons, I think about whether I should try calling him again. I could offer to get on a train, to be with him in Yorkshire, but I don't even know how ill his nan is, or if they are even close. I'm still getting used to being in love and what you are supposed to do or say, to show that you love them, but not show it too much. All I know about his family's place in Yorkshire is that it is where he goes 'to decompress' and where he stores all his CDs and swimming trophies, not that I've seen them. When I call, he doesn't answer, but I don't leave a message for fear of saying the wrong thing.

Once I'm inside the pub, the music is loud and the windows have steamed up, making it easy to forget about the world outside. There is a whole bunch of us by now, maybe six or seven, crammed into two wooden benches around a wooden table, drinking pints. It's one of those pubs that looks like the inside of an arc. At closing time, the barman opens the big wooden double-doors and we spill out into the street, but no one wants to go home, so I say we can all go back to my room. I thought it was a very generous thing to say.

All I have to offer everyone is a pack of six white bread rolls, which we all enjoy because we're pissed. We put on music and eat and smoke Marlboro Lights and I make them vodka and oranges whilst listening to everyone talk loudly, and I realise that my body is starting to relax. At some point in the night, two of my friends start getting off with each other, on a chair in the corner. Two more of my friends have also paired off now. It was quite normal back then for a situation to become charged with sexual energy, abruptly, as we all lived in a state of near constant sexual tension. At first, I just watched everyone rolling around, kissing and laughing on my bed, sat with my back to the wall, holding my knees to my chest. A beautiful boy with dark circles under his eyes, who I knew a bit, asked if he could kiss me and I said yes. Afterwards he said, 'You're a good kisser,' and I've never, ever forgotten that. It's great to be told that you are good at something at a relatively young age, it always stays with you.

It was quiet, no one was really talking now, just the sound of Bowie on the stereo. The thrill of kissing someone, in the proximity of someone else.

A handsome, humourless boy, who didn't usually hang out with us, suddenly said, 'Bowie would've approved of this,' and everyone cringed a bit at what he'd said. It slightly ruined the atmosphere. For me, it was something about the word 'this'.

I felt a cake tin touching my feet when I woke up, the next morning, alone in my bed. The lid was on tight, but it was uncomfortable and sharp, digging into my ankle bone. The tin had a pattern all around it like Russian folk art. This tin had been in my family for as long as I could remember. I never saw it being used as a cake tin though, but whenever I looked inside there were crumbs at the bottom, so someone must have, at some point. Perhaps my nan. For some unknown reason, when I was packing to go to university, my mum put the tin out for me to take, which I did. But I hadn't cooked in the whole time I'd been a student. I kept the tin in my room, to use as an ashtray. It was particularly handy for visitors.

When my first love got back, he didn't have a clue what had happened, not even when my friends and I all contracted the same throat infection from all the smoking and kissing.

'How is your nan?' I asked.

'Yeah, fine. It was a false alarm. What did you do when I was away?' he asked.

'I went out for a bit and then came back and did my *Medea* essay,' I said.

He absent-mindedly picked up the Russian cake tin and felt its weight, which made him want to open it. When he did, he shouted, 'Jesus! That's fucking rank!'

It was full of cigarette butts. Imagine! A cake tin full of cigarette butts. It stank.

'That's not just me,' I said defensively, 'I've had a lot of people in my room.'

'When?' he said.

'A few nights ago.'

'Who was here?'

So I told him and described the whole night to him and the part where we all started kissing. When I got to the end of the story, I said, 'Are you jealous?'

'Why would I be jealous?' he said.

We weren't together, he was my first love, but he didn't know it, and I never told him.

When you love someone, it's hard to accept that they don't love you. It's hard to think that the love only matters to you and that the love doesn't even exist outside of your body.

I sat on my bed, looking up at him, holding the cigarette cake tin away from his body.

A few years later, when we did actually sleep together, I was waiting for some kind of revelation, but the reality of being with him was kind of boring and embarrassing, really. As I lay there in the dim light of his bedside lamp, I was distracted by my split ends.

It was only later that week, at the hairdresser's when the split ends were being cut off, that I concluded that it was best as a fantasy relationship, not a real one. And there were no feelings after that, as if the love had only lived in the ends of my hair.

10

SIX CAKES AND SIX MUCH SMALLER CAKES

My friend wrote music. She was impressive and pretty and wore the right bands on T-shirts. We first met working in a shitty call centre in Cardiff. I was fired first, and wore it like a badge of honour. On our cigarette breaks, we talked about her band, her obese mum and *The Bell Jar*. She wanted her band to be more like the band Hole but the other bandmates were too laid back. I would look at her heavy black fringe and lip ring and worry that, in contrast, I looked like a trainee teacher. And now we had ended up in London around the same time and both at twenty-six. She invited me to go to a music awards ceremony, not a very impressive one, but I was still excited and intimidated. I spent the next few days browsing shops, picking out dresses that my mum would've called 'too revealing', then putting them back on the rails. I thought about how they would look on Facebook. Everything ended up on Facebook, especially bad outfits. Eventually I picked a crushed-velvet dress that was short, but with a high neck and long, wing-like sleeves, a choice made by the memory of my mother's words: 'Show leg or cleavage, never both.' I knew that I'd have to starve myself for at least a week to fit into the dress, and when the night came to put it on, the starving had worked. But as I stood up to get my coat, my bedroom moved in a slow circle, one way, then the other – I guess my blood sugar was so low.

It was the fact that you were supposed to look your best at things like awards ceremonies that I found stressful. I much preferred compliments when I wasn't striving to look nice. But as soon as I got to the party I was relieved to find that people still looked like themselves, just in slightly nicer clothes, even though I hadn't seen any of them before. Before I moved to London, I had this naive notion that it was full of beautiful people, just walking around outside Topshop, waiting to be scouted by a model agent.

I had met him a few times before, in a bar once that was red, in King's Cross. I remember him being funny and him thinking I was funny, but I didn't fancy him at all. The party took place in a big hall. It was too noisy to talk, so we went with him and his friends on to the smoking balcony. He discreetly took a swig from a monogrammed hip flask (that he probably got for passing his driving test or something) before placing it back in his shirt pocket.

My friend and I shared a cigarette. Hip Flask took our photograph, with her doing a thumbs up, shivering in her corset, and me playing an invisible flute with my mouth, to make my cheeks higher and fuller (something I had learnt from a beauty segment on *This Morning*). He paid more attention to my friend than to me, and seemed really into her. I spoke to one of his friends – a small woman with a mean face, who told me that she had been a background extra in the orgy scene in *Eyes Wide Shut*, and did I want to hear all about it?

All the free champagne had gone by the time we had got there – we had spent so long getting ready – so Hip Flask bought us a couple of rounds. He was a bit older and seemed like he had more money than us, so we let him. My friend kept saying what a great guy he was and that they were going to work together on something, but I didn't know what he did. 'Yeah, he seems really cool,' I agreed. I thought maybe my friend was going to go home with him, and I tried to remember what night bus I would need to get if I was going to be travelling home without her. There was no way I could have afforded a cab.

Because of my very empty stomach, the alcohol instantly made me funnier, louder and more opiniated, which Hip Flask seemed to enjoy. I told him the story of how I got fired from the banking call centre: 'They thought something was wrong with my phone . . . they sent a tech guy round, like, three times to look at it, but in reality I was just panicking and hanging up on customers. I hadn't listened during training, and I didn't know how to do anything, apart from change customers' addresses . . .' He laughed and put his arm around my friend's shoulder, keeping her warm.

People were starting to leave. My friend wanted to carry on partying. We had formed a small group by now: us, Hip Flask, Eyes Wide Shut and her mate. We went to two more bars, and the night kept going in the way that the telling of a joke can't be stopped once it's started. Hip Flask invited us all back to his place. We all piled into a taxi together. Hip Flask was doing that thing where you say, 'This is how you work out your porn name, you take your first . . .' which was the sort of thing you find funny when you don't have much imagination. *Maybe I've misremembered him having a good sense of humour,* I thought to myself. I was starting to feel sick, but was too drunk to care, or think about work the next day.

His whole flat was dark. We sat around in his dingy living room, snacking on the crisps we'd found in his cupboards, whilst he skinned up. 'Oh, they're my flatmate's crisps,' he said, annoyed, but the flatmate wasn't there, so he didn't really care. At the time, he seemed so grown up. On the sofa, he told a story about being mugged in Brixton, and when I said, 'Oh my God, poor you,' he touched my knee and said, 'I'm fine now though.' There was talk of getting pizza, but no one took the initiative. Eyes Wide Shut handed round a picture of herself, on her BlackBerry, semi-naked on the set of *Eyes Wide Shut.* My friend and Hip Flask got into a heated discussion about pubic hair after that, in which I recall Hip Flask trying to win the argument by loudly saying, 'But it's just NICER for the guy, it's just a NICER experience for the guy, the less hair there is.'

I threw up a small amount of sick in his bathroom and squeezed some of his, or his flatmate's, toothpaste on to my finger and rubbed it on my gums like coke. When I came back out, I quickly realised that my friend had gone home with Eyes Wide Shut – to see the naked photo in 3D. It was just me and Hip Flask. I stood by the large bookshelves, sipping some water out of an enamel mug, and tried to think straight, plan my journey home. 'Whereabouts are we?' I said, but he was too focused on skinning up again to answer. I scanned the shelves, as if looking for help. There was nothing unexpected: cacti, vinyl, *Pulp Fiction*, *The God Delusion*, a Philip Roth, a postcard of Stonehenge, pictures of a sister maybe and *Harry Potter*. He came over to me and calmly took the mug out of my hand and said, 'You can just crash on the sofa.' It looked cold and dark outside and I was so tired. Everything would be easier in the morning, and I would wake up very early and go home to change out of my dress, before work. I curled up on the sofa and he disappeared into his room. It was about an hour later that the harsh fluorescent glow of the bathroom light woke me up. As Hip Flask made his way back through the living room, to his bedroom, he saw that I was awake and said, 'It's silly you being out here, when there's a bed.' I obediently followed him into his plain room. It seemed to make logical sense, and I was too tired to care. I don't remember what I thought might happen, but I didn't think it meant a green light to anything. I wanted to sleep.

I was lying on my back, but with my head turned away from him, the dress restricting the tops of my arms a little. I saw the loud baggy shirt that he'd worn at the party hanging on the back of an IKEA chair. I remember placing my bracelet on the bedside table and noticing an old-fashioned landline telephone, and thinking it so urbane. I could smell his aftershave. I didn't know what it was called, but it was a popular scent at the time. He kissed my neck and it made me jump. His lips felt dry and warm. I always believed the onus was on me to turn down men gently, so as not to offend, or cause a fuss, or be seen as too sensitive, or provoke anger. I turned my head and gently said, 'I didn't come here for that.' He reached down and put his hand there. 'Your body says otherwise,' he said. I felt shocked, but also as though I had just lost an argument. It seemed that this was some sort of debate, as if my body suddenly belonged to both of us. Because he had touched me there, a line had been crossed – I had no idea that once something became sexual, you shouldn't really change your mind, or that made you a 'prick-tease'. You couldn't just stop, in the way that the telling of a joke can't be stopped once it's started. I felt so silly, so naive – what did I expect, if I was going to get into a bed with a man in just his boxers? I suppose my silence was the willingness he needed. I lay there and let him get on with it. It felt as though it was easier to just get it over with, so I could sleep. But it was more than that: confusion and anxiety had caused my throat to close off. I'd never been less present in my body. His dick felt small, about the size of a Tracker bar. I thought, *How have I got myself here?* I counted the thrusts. No big deal, just drunk sex, nothing special, nothing new – don't make a fuss. I wanted to seem mature and sorted and streetwise and like a city person.

He moved back to his side of the bed. And I was left looking up at the recessed ceiling lights. I hadn't even thought he fancied me.

My friend Lydia once said, 'We've all had sex with men

that we didn't want to have sex with. If I hadn't gone along with it, they might have done it anyway.'

I was raised on the sexual politics of musicals, so I'm screwed, whatever. In particular, I didn't know how to speak up, or speak out, with men. As a result, 'invisible things ... happened between us that night'.* Hip Flask didn't want to think about this unspoken exchange: I wasn't able to communicate what I didn't want as easily as he could communicate what he did want. This is what happens, if you've been body-shamed from a young age: you lose the ability to feel as though your body is your own. You muddle your needs with someone else's very easily, because you don't think your body is worth defending. And I didn't know how to articulate any of this to Hip Flask, at 3 a.m. Would he even have listened? In all honesty, I felt too fat to say no.

In the morning, I woke up with an anxious feeling in my stomach and made the short walk to the bathroom. I didn't have enough time to go home – I would have to go to work in this stupid dress. I blew my nose, quietly – I didn't want to wake him. I've had sinus problems ever since I was accidentally hit in the face with a bag of flour when I was six, during a panto starring a famous 80s comedian. Sometimes red wine makes the inside of my nose swell up and become blocked. Water or pale piss had pooled on the tiled floor, just beside the loo. I noticed a copy of *The Game* on the windowsill, but turned away, as if it were an

---

* Kaitlin Prest, from her audio series 'No'

embarrassing childhood photo. I know how this goes, he would have bought it ironically, read it sincerely. I thought back to earlier on in the night, when he had ignored me, and just spoken to my friend. Maybe this was a technique? The one where you subtly insult women into bed. I turned on the tap to wash my face and water splashed on the book and I thought, *Good*. I brushed my teeth with my finger. When I came out of the bathroom, he was already up, scrambling eggs, and that's when I felt the first flash of anger. It was something about his over-confident manner. He asked me if I wanted any. I said no and watched him take a plate of food into the living room. I stayed in the hallway but could hear him eating. It sounded like he was swallowing mud.

'I've got orange juice, if you want it?' he shouted. I went into the kitchen, opened the fridge and looked at the orange juice. There was a box of six cupcakes on the middle fridge shelf, maybe a gift. I took one of the cakes, quickly wrapped it in kitchen roll and put it in my bag. 'I'm going,' I said. He stood up and walked towards me. I thought maybe he was going to check I was all right, but he tried to kiss me goodbye. That's when I realised that we had very different versions of the night before. He seemed unaware that I had been uncomfortable with what had taken place between us. The kiss was telling me the story that this had been fun for both of us.

I left, feeling rough, almost tripping over a recycling box full of old newspapers in the hall outside his door.

Still drunk, I ate the cupcake on the Tube, surrounded by a sea of workers dressed in blues, blacks and greys. I looked around, repeatedly checking that I wasn't going the wrong way on the Circle Line, as I often did. In the city I was always getting lost, always moving, never still, always broke and sleep deprived. But leaving would seem like a life in reverse, like I was going backwards.

I looked at the unwanted bulge in my stomach and tried to cover it up with my bag. If I could just make my body smaller, firmer, then I would be protected from things like this happening again. A thin body conveyed restraint, self-worth, and no one would think to abuse it. I believed thinness was a protection from misuse and harm. Society stands up for the thin body.

The boy sat next to me was in a T-shirt and jeans with so much gel in his hair he looked like he'd just been swimming. He was falling asleep with his head dangling down. He smelt of beer and bubble gum, the latter was maybe on account of the open can of Red Bull in his hand. His body fell against mine, so that our shoulders were touching. I let him sleep, too bloated from the carbohydrate to care or move, but was careful that the can didn't spill on me. My dress looked different in the bright lights of the Circle Line, more boring, less dressy. Thank God I didn't choose a 'revealing dress' and had heeded my mother's advice.

I was there, but not there, finishing off the last bit of cake.

I came to enjoy city life in the same way that people enjoy horror films: adrenally.

The director looked like a lumberjack and didn't seem to mind that I was ten minutes late or wearing a formal dress and heels to my first day of rehearsals. It was my second or third television job, acting in a sitcom for one of the lesser-watched channels. I stood around sipping coffee from a paper cup with a few of the other actors. 'I love your dress,' one of the older women said to me. 'Thank you,' I said almost inaudibly, trying to pull a face which would look like I wasn't still drunk. She eyed my unbrushed hair and smiled politely. The director was drinking from a Coke bottle and moving plastic chairs about the hall. It was really cold. Thankfully, I had also packed a cardigan with me the night before, but it had a large bow on the front and I didn't like wearing it after that night – I felt it made me look like a big present. If I hadn't been so broke, I think I would have feigned illness and left the rehearsal hall, but I knew I had to stay.

In the first scene we rehearsed, we were a group of beauticians on the piss. One of the other actors, about my age, had to say the line, 'Ooh, I forgot to put me knickers on.' The director, who liked to make a tent shape with his fingers whilst directing, laughed loudly. An Afghan hound, belonging to the producer, got excited every time the director laughed, and yelped for about ten seconds. The producer would put his hand down to stroke its head and say, 'Shuuush.' After I said my line, I glanced at the dog, anxiously – half expecting it to laugh, but it didn't. We did it again, but this time when my friend said, 'Ooh, I forgot to put me knickers on,' the older woman turned to the director and said, 'You do know she [pointing at the actor whose line it was] has a first from Cambridge, don't you?'

The actor laughed, a little embarrassed. 'We can't make her say that!?' the woman continued. It wasn't clear who was joking and who was wasn't, but the director laughed into his chest and the dog stood up. 'I don't mind saying it,' the actor said. 'Actually,' the director said, 'it would make *more* sense if you take the next line, because you're the one who goes to the bar ... so we can use that to cover your exit, d'youseewhatImean? Ummmm, so ... Katy, if you say it, instead?' I couldn't think of anything witty to say, so I just said, 'Yep, OK, I can do that.' We did the scene again. 'Ooh, I forgot to put my knickers on,' I said when it was my turn to speak. The dog left the room.

At least, I was earning more than at the call centre. At least, I was being paid to express myself in some way, even if it wasn't the art I had imagined. At least, I could be creative.

We moved on to the next scene. The director moved the chairs again, so that they resembled the layout of a bus. I didn't have any lines in this one – I just had to react. I was bored and began to daydream about the time my English grandfather saw me in a play in Cardiff and afterwards pronounced that I had been good, but 'wasn't attractive enough to be on television'. In the daydream version of him, there is icing dripping down his head.

I shared some of the Tube ride home with one of the executive producers, who helpfully told me that I was 'too in-between' and that 'no one would know what to cast me as'. I looked confused at this. 'Looks-wise, you're too in-between – you need to put on loads of weight or lose loads of weight,' he clarified for me.

My friend posted pictures from that evening on Facebook. When I saw the one of my friend and me, her shivering in her corset, I studied my face to try to remember how I had been feeling at the start of the night. I was the only one in the photo with a large bag. I've never owned a small purse, the type you take to events, and I've never really understood the concept of enjoying a bag. I 'like' the photo. I won't tell my friend how the evening had ended. It would be too complicated.

I didn't think again about that evening until several months later, when my English grandfather died. My dearest friend, B, took me out for dinner. B took a close interest in my emotional welfare. She had been the only one of my friends, for example, who had offered to have my English grandfather killed for me, when he was alive. She knew people, or her cousin knew people – it wasn't an impossibility. I was very touched. She took me seriously. It's a wonderful feeling, knowing that someone is so completely on your side, without agenda.

When my mother told me on the phone that he had died, I didn't know how to comfort her. I didn't have the words or the maturity, I suppose. It's something I've always felt guilty about.

I was so thrilled to be seeing B. I started to feel better just by being around her. When our pizzas arrived, they were put down on placemats, with pictures of the same pizza on, but nicer. B and I had become friends because on our first day at university we were wearing almost the same jacket, but I thought hers was nicer. She was the first female I had met who owned a private collection of bongs. By now, the show had gone out on telly at eleven thirty at night. 'We watched, but your father fell asleep,' my mother had said to me the following day. Thankfully, the 'Ooh, I forgot to put me knickers on' scene hadn't made the final show.

Our conversation was interrupted by someone placing something sparkly on our table. I slowly looked up from my pizza. It was not immediately obvious that it was him, because he had chopped off his jaw-length hair, but I remembered the scent. 'Hey,' he said, smiling. 'I think this belongs to you. I've had it in my bag for ages.' It was my silver bracelet. He spoke slightly too loudly, as if in a play. I remember puzzling over the bracelet at first, because it looked different, somehow, less sparkly. He tried to make conversation, but I just thanked him abruptly and then began drinking water quickly, trying to wash it all away. He said that he had to go. He turned to leave, then yelled out, 'I'm having a party by the way.' He went over to join a girl at the bar who looked a bit like him. They both kept their backs to us for the rest of the night.

'Do you have any chocolate cake?' I asked the waiter.

When the cake arrived, B said it was 'dry and a bit shit'.

'Do you think he's been carrying it around, all this time, then, like just in his backpack? It doesn't make sense.'

B sent the cake back, which was an inspiration – it had never occurred to me to send a cake back because it was a bit dry and shit.

*   *   *

My amazing toy oven was dinky with a black hob and two hooks on the side for utensils. There was just room for six red rubber cakes to fit on to the plastic shelf inside. I would cook them over and over again. I knew they weren't real, but I loved going along with it, each time. I was six. The oven was portable enough to be carried with me to my English grandparents' house, and when I picked it up, I would feel the plastic seam that ran along the bottom. When we bought the oven, the man at the store threw in the sixth red-rubber cake for free and winked at me. When I got home, I wrote out several recipes on pieces of paper and stapled them together to make a recipe book. The ingredients consisted of things that had been left on the floor and so within my eyeline: coins, pencils, receipts, hair. I like to think of these recipes really as my first poems.

The corridor at my English grandparents' house was long with a grandfather clock at one end. A green-and-white floral carpet covered the floor, but when I played on it, up close, the flowers looked like cabbages. When you closed the oven door and put the timer on, a small light came on inside. The timer only went up to thirty seconds. When the light broke, I would stick my head right inside the oven, and it was the same darkness as the one in our living room, when Dad would draw the curtains before an afternoon kids' film on TV. I often think that microwaves are the grown-up equivalent of toy ovens. Once, when I put my cardigan in the oven, my English grandma, as she was cleaning the oven door for me, said, 'Clothes, in the oven?' I would think about this years later, when in my Welsh oral exam I accidentally said,

'I get dressed in the kitchen,' and the Welsh teacher snorted and exclaimed, '*Yn y gegin*? In the kitchen?' My English grandmother was a sweet woman, short and glamorous, and always humming to herself.

I remember my English grandfather's leather slippers, which looked like two big tongues, coming into view. He trod on one or two of my recipes, ripping them, then looked annoyed and said, 'Move out of the way, piggy.' At first, I wasn't sure what had happened, because I liked pigs, but as I cleared everything away I realised what he had meant: pigs ate too much and were disgusting and fat.

Why this adult couldn't bear to see such an idyllic scene, and so ruined it, I'll never fully understand.

I'll never know why my English grandad did what he did. What his obsession with my appearance was really about. The incident with the oven was how I found out that there was something deeply wrong and unlovable about my body. Sadly, it felt like the end of innocence. My body was now a battleground – and the war would go on for thousands of hours and cost me thousands of pounds in therapeutic strategies.

The first time I slept with a man that I felt an overwhelming physical attraction to, I was about twenty-nine. Up until then, it was more to do with feeling safe. He was younger than me, which finally gave me the authority I had always longed for. I was attracted to his shyness and cleverness. We had kissed late at night, after eating free gateaux at a party, and we tasted of cigarettes and cherries. It started as a joke at first: I said that I would go home with him, but only because I needed to use his printer – no one owned printers in the noughties. But then, once we were in his room, he was so eager and nervous. When I told him to slow down and savour the moment, he looked at me like I was a prophet. For a brief moment, we were stopped in time, like figures on an urn. I was the one with all the power, and it had to stay that way, in order for the dynamic to work. I sensed that the moment I showed too much vulnerability, it would fail. It felt good to be involved in my own desire.

I thought about him all the time. It was difficult to concentrate at work. I wanted to be in love, but also didn't, because love is a type of madness, and I wasn't feeling emotionally stable enough to be mad.

One night, when he was running late, I was in a pub chatting to his housemate.

'The landlord won't do anything about it. Sorry, is this boring?' he said.

'No, I had mice once,' I replied.

'Yeah, so they live behind – oh, wait, have you been to our place?'

I didn't answer, just gave him a tight smile. I had never seen any of the housemates when I had been at my young man's place, not out of secrecy, it had just never happened. But this meant that he had never mentioned me being there. It hurt a little, to be so absent. I felt like a mistress for some reason, or old and silly. The young man appeared out of nowhere, looking pleased to see me. It began to crumble after that. I finally walked away for good, and down an escalator. We were in a shopping centre at the time. He said that he didn't love me but that he had an intense admiration for me. Which, now, seems actually nice, but at the time was kind of devastating. I paid for two teas and then held his gaze on the descending escalator until I couldn't see him.

A few weeks later, I went on a holiday to southern Spain, with friends. I was OK – sad, but OK – which isn't the same as *real* heartbreak at all. But I kept feeling the need to look at everything he was doing on social media. It was only when I returned home and saw my bill from Orange that it all felt so masochistic.

In our Spanish villa, my friends and I watched something on TV about Britney's recent breakdown. Shots of her shaved head were intercut with therapists, enlightened looking, in front of bookshelves, performing surgery on her pain. They were fluent in the effects and symptoms of fame. But it was mere conjecture. They didn't really know her or what happened. They didn't have any real knowledge of Britney's health. They wouldn't know, for example, if Britney's meds gave her diarrhoea.

The few years I spent on an SSRI seem strangely shallow and vague when I try to recall them, as if all that extra serotonin stopped new memories from being formed. But it was a necessity to take them. The first time I took antidepressants, I found it depressing, because it worked so well. It confirmed just how acclimatised I had become to my own depression, that it only appeared to me once I had taken a pill to stop it. It seemed depressing that perspective was just a small chemical adjustment to the brain. But, then, depression is depressing.

For some reason, when I decided to come off the medication I did it during a long run of a play. I had sweats and brain-zaps in front of a thousand people every night, on stage, but I don't think anyone noticed. Once the drugs were out of my system, I suddenly realised that the play was really bad.

The first time I thought about medication, but didn't do anything about it, I was around twenty-three and working in the home section of a department store. It was boring but easy. I was less bored on the days that Carl was there, a nervous freckly guy who was easy to get on with. Most times he would talk about which members of staff he hated, the meaning of certain lyrics and his favourite quotes from *Blue Jam*. We would volunteer to fold the towels together, which should've taken half an hour but could be stretched out to an hour if you were smart. We had a sort of unsaid agreement between us: we would try and do as little work as possible and this was our secret.

The shop required us to work in four-hour shifts, with fifteen-minute breaks in between, but the break room was on the top floor of the building. Customers would stop me and ask for help, on my way through the store and up the stairs. I would try to pretend I wasn't staff, by covering my name badge with folded arms, but the uniforms were garish and obvious. Carl's accent was a mix of Spanish and Cardiff, and he switched between the two voices, depending on what he was talking about. We had started at the same time. The training was done all together, in one big group, each of us insisting that we were going to be the worst, making little jokes. At the end of the training, all everyone wanted to know was: where could we smoke, and could we take the about-to-go-off food home, for free?

I let out a yelp one day in the stockroom, when a mouse had become stuck to some flypaper. The stockroom, to my surprise, had beautiful acoustics. The mouse had tried to pull its body off, and there was a smear of blood where it had dragged itself and the paper into a corner. Carl had to kill it. Afterwards, I was so full of adrenaline that I spoke non-stop for forty-five minutes:

'Did you do the *Mabinogion* at school, Carl?'

'No. I mean yes, why?'

'Do you remember the story where a guy tries to hang a mouse?'

'Yeah.'

'Because one night he sees an army of mice attacking his crops, and he chases them, but they're really fast, apart from this one fat one that is slow?'

'Yeah.'

'And then he puts the fat mouse in his glove and then he's so angry that he decides to hang it for stealing. He sticks two forks in the ground on top of a hill, then adds the little crossbar, across the top, and ties a rope around the mouse's neck, but then, just at the last moment, a bishop appears and says, "No, that's my wife. She was pregnant, and I turned her into a mouse"?'

'Yeah.'

But I knew he didn't know that story.

Then, at Christmas, I was moved to the food hall, with its big fake garlands, elf hats and pissed-up office workers buying South African wines at 8 p.m. I stacked pigs-in-blankets and crackers and cream cakes and checked sell-by dates, in four-hour shifts.

I made a new friend, with dyed red hair, like the red of a Comic Relief nose. She worked part-time, to fund her Fine Art degree. Even now, if I smell bacon, I will think of her saying, 'Next year, for my final piece, I'm going to have a bare room with a single, naked light bulb, with a strip of bacon wrapped around it, cooking.' It was one of the most profound ideas I'd ever heard.

I first noticed him when he was staring at me as I put out the eclairs. It was distracting and he made me feel nervous so that the cake boxes became sweaty in my hands. He had appeared from one of the staff doors at the side of the food hall and just hovered there. I thought maybe he was assessing my performance, but he had nothing in his hand like a piece of paper or a pen or a clipboard.

Customers would pick up a cake, and then leave it some-where else, and I had to put them back in their right place. The cakes sort of called to each other, so it was easy to find them. I saw him there by the door, again, a few days later. When I looked up at him, suddenly he seemed kind of frozen but maybe it was the stress of middle management.

One day, in the staff canteen, I made my friend with the

red hair observe him as I put my lunch tray back. 'Did he look?' I said. 'Yes,' she said, 'he watched you the whole way there and back,' and I felt a tiny bit excited and nervous. A married man wanted me.

The staring went on for days, until I was drunk enough to say hello to him at the Christmas staff do. At first, he seemed very professional. Then, later, sat in the corner of a rugby-themed pub, we kissed, and he told me what he wanted to do to me.

I didn't see him again for several weeks, until a stressed-looking co-worker suddenly appeared next to me, as if she had fallen from the sky, and told me to follow her. We went into one of the small back rooms. The married man was stood up, in his navy suit. A young woman had been caught shoplifting. She was silent, resting her elbows on the table, in the middle of the room, in a white jumper and leggings. She was staring just ahead and down, in sombre concentration, as if looking at a gravestone.

That's why I was needed – as a witness. I was relieved. I thought they knew, that I was going to be sacked. The married man and I didn't look at each other, so as not to acknowledge the erotics in the room. The co-worker said that the police were on their way and I believed her. Sometimes the staff just said that to scare teenagers who had shoplifted something small. The woman in the white jumper looked at me imploringly. She had smuggled things down her leggings, which had perfectly retained their shape, like in a cartoon, when a snake swallows something: I could see the shape of a small bottle of wine and a DVD. On the table in front of her were a few other items that she must have nicked as well, like bread, custard tarts and a chocolate Santa. I felt oddly proud that she taken one of the cakes from my display. I always tried to straighten out the dents in the packaging before they were just chucked away, as faulty – it was like animal rescue work. I wanted her to have the cake so much, and I was sad that she had been caught.

The married man continued to look at me, but from afar.

If I hadn't read *Fat Is A Feminist Issue* by Susie Orbach or anything by Geneen Roth, I would have never healed my relationship with food. These books introduced me to the concept of intuitive eating. I didn't know what my natural appetite was – always lurching from one state of fullness back to emptiness. I just didn't trust myself or my body. It began with stopping starving and understanding that the food wasn't going to go anywhere – no one was going to take it away, or say I couldn't have it. At first, I exalted in fat and all the 'banned' foods from my childhood. It seemed to horrify people, the idea that I was deliberately allowing myself to get bigger. Costume departments shamed me, people asked me if I was all right. It felt like the wildest and most rebellious act imaginable. But I knew that fixing this relationship was more important to me than how I looked. I stopped joining in with conversations about weight with other women. I know it's a boring female paradigm, that women self-critique to bond, but some conversations ran dry very quickly. I stopped insulting my body, and when I did I would immediately apologise to it. For so many years, I was too scared to eat any fat. As a result, little red spots appeared all over my dry body, and my periods became irregular.

After years of being in a toxic relationship with food, the doctors told me that I would need to have my gall bladder removed, because it was infected and inflamed. They couldn't say for certain whether my disordered eating had been a contributing factor. The feeling in my body told me that it was.

My relationship with food was a little like my relationship with men: I craved that which was wrong for me, until it lost its allure altogether.

To summarise: never trust a man who has a landline next to his bed.

11

DOLL CAKE, OR, THREE DOLLS I HAVE MET

First

When I did work experience in the clocks and watches department in a Welsh museum, there was one clock that used to freak me out. The clock would announce each hour with a wooden boy and girl, who would pop out of a small door, then vanish back in again. But I got used to them, and then, on the last day, I was allowed to clean them, with a cotton bud. The dolls had waited a long time to be cleaned, because dust floated off their little hipster clothes.

I must have been around fifteen. It was an odd choice for work experience, but all the other placements had gone, so it was either clocks or a garden centre, because I had ticked the box saying 'yes' to 'working outside'. So now, for a whole week, it would just be me, the clocks and the clockmaker: a stout man in his sixties with a reddish beard.

When he let me in, each day, I would smile and say good morning, and he would say, 'I suppose you want Radio One on, do yer?'

He spent ages fixing this one antique clock on the first day. After a while he looked up and said, 'I'm totally self-taught, you know.' I nodded. He spent the whole week working on that same clock. It made me wonder if he thought he would keel over from a heart attack once he'd mended it, like it was keeping him alive.

I quite enjoyed all the intense ticking in the room. It was like we were being timed.

From the moment I found out about death I began to see people as clocks. I was a clock, I came from a family of clocks. Photos began to resemble groups of clocks. 'Clocks stop when they want, you see,' the man suddenly said.

The boys I liked were all covered in prehistoric mud. They were out-of-work actors and students who sat in the replica Iron Age roundhouse, based on some actual remains. Their job was to squat inside the hut, gathered around the cooking pot, to show visitors what life would have looked like back then, back before clocks. At lunchtime, they would down tools and head to the canteen. From my work bench, I could see them through the window, in their robes and tunics, with their long hair and muddied arms. They looked like an indie band. I would then go for my lunch, so that I could sit behind them and fancy them and listen to their conversations as I unfurled my pudding.

Second

When I presented my friend with the doll cake I had (iron-ically) made for her birthday, she looked as though her heart had stopped for a second. Later, when we were alone, at her kitchen table, she said, 'When I was young, my mum made me the same one. It was a way of trying to distract me from Dad's behaviour.'

I had made it by placing a Barbie upright in the middle, so that the cake part resembled a big heavy skirt. Now it sat in between us, half eaten. Everyone else had gone by now. I could see one of Barbie's legs exposed through the sponge. It was a significant birthday for my friend, a significant age.

She told me how much she had hated her childhood Barbies, and how it was her mum who had bought them for her, because her mum liked them, not her. How, even though she was long and lean, like her Barbie (because she had danced from a young age), Barbie had big tits, which she didn't, pink skin, which she didn't, and straight hair, which she didn't. But most of all she was jealous of her doll's incorruptibility. My friend doesn't remember ever feeling innocent, even as a child. The whole family knew about the affair straight away. After her dad moved out, she found that her sense of balance wasn't as good, which eventually meant that she wasn't top of the class any more in her dance lessons.

We sat in silence looking at the cake, drinking wine. When

I lifted the Barbie up, her high-heeled shoe dropped off. I'd forgotten that, underneath, Barbie's feet are moulded into the shape of a heel. She has been built for heels.

Everyone has the right to own a doll that looks like them.

Third

The woman leading the workshop laid out the cloth bodies, which we would have to stuff. We were all sat close to each other on plastic chairs around a trestle table. Once we had stuffed our dolls, it was time to decorate them so they looked like us. Then we carried them around the house all day. The therapist running the body-positivity course said they represented us, but as children, and they would tell her everything she needed to know about how we felt about ourselves: you dropped your doll on the floor and it almost got decapitated by the patio doors? 'Very interesting,' the therapist would say. You are squeezing the doll too tight? You are dragging her by the foot? You left her in the toilet? You've got your arm over her mouth? 'All very useful information,' the therapist would say.

The next day (because this was a hard-core, stay-over-for-three-nights course in a house in Kent), we had to talk about what we had learnt from the exercise. A woman called Pia said, 'I should have made my doll fatter. I was a fat kid.'

'Then why didn't you?' someone else said, which made Pia go red.

'Even though I'm thin now,' she said, 'I forget. Even

though I've had the gastric band fitted, I know that when people meet me, they can tell I used to be fat . . . because . . . I have fat eyes.' There was something extremely sad about Pia as she said this.

Then we had an hour to write a list of all the things that we can remember people have said to us about our bodies. I wrote continually, without stopping: you are the right size, not too big or too small, you cannot waste a body like that, you're big, but I'd still fuck you, nice and curvy, I thought you were an apple shape, but you're actually a brick, your neck is too short to play a Shakespearian heroine, your eyelashes are really sparsely populated, nice and big, you're so tiny, I'd love to wake up next to your body, but my wife wouldn't let me, I didn't touch you – I don't know what you're talking about – you hold yourself with the confidence of a much smaller woman, you are bigger than the women I would usually go for, but confidence is always attractive, you have eyelashes like a foreign person, please tell me you're not wearing that, didn't you have time to shave? These nice little dresses aren't for you, I'm afraid, your big clothes are over there, you're actually quite small in that area, maybe wait till you're smaller, grief obviously suits you, you're shrinking, we're not saying you're fat, obviously, just fashion-fat, fat in the world of fashion, oh, I just assumed you would want your arms covered up, is all, why have you lost weight – I hope you're still funny, you're tall, are you tall? Do you use conditioner? Is that a scar? Smile more, you're not conventionally attractive but I fancy you, chunky, flabby, solid, masculine, feminine, is that muscle? Well done, it fits, don't stand like that, you're not going to be able to hide yourself, you're too big, you could even out your eyebrows, your face is too round, breathe in, and so on and so on.

By the time we had all read out our lists, everyone was crying, silently. After a while, Pia said, 'I want to say something,' and everyone turned to face her. 'I get a cake mix, the packet ones, when you just add eggs and water. And I make the cake and then when it's cooled I cut it into four, then I liquidise it, bit by bit, and drink it, so that it doesn't burst my new smaller stomach.'

The therapist said, 'Addiction is the strongest force in the universe, Pia. It will always find a way.'

I nodded sagely, but what I was sarcastically thinking was, surely not stronger than gravity? But, years later, when I got to witness the effects of addiction, up close, I understood what the therapist had meant and regretted my cynicism.

At the end of the course, the therapist said that we could take our dolls home with us if we wanted. No one did.

12

BARA BRITH,
OR,
WALKING WITH MY FATHER

My first memory of him is holding his calloused hand as I bent down to inspect some bird tracks along the frozen river. As I looked up at him, he looked as tall as the trees behind him. There was snow on both.

That the story begins and ends with snow is so appropriate because snow is quiet and sad, like this story.

Snow doesn't stay on the earth for long.

It was a wood, but we called it a forest, like when we said, 'Shall we go up to the forest on Sunday?'

The forest was near to our house, but we always drove. Dad took me there more often than Mum did. I would sit in the front of the car and point at tractors and houses that were very tall and the cottages that were cute and say, 'That's where I'll live when I'm older.' When I was around eight, Dad joked that I could go and live in one now and I said, 'But I don't want to,' and that night I wailed in my sleep because a giant rabbit had drowned both my parents in a huge bucket. We walked even when it was raining, and it was raining most of the time, regularly flooding the banks of the River Ely. There was one very hot summer I do remember though, because they filmed an episode of a Welsh soap opera in the car park of our local pub. Dad and I drove past it and he tutted. When I watched the episode on telly, it looked like it had been shot in Marbella, not the outskirts of Cardiff, the sun was so white, like I half expected a gecko to crawl across the shot.

Retirees outnumbered children in the village. There was an innocence to the place, but darkness too if you knew where to look for it: discovering a sheep skull at the side of a lane, spying a scrap of pornography discarded in a hedgerow. And there was always that one house in a village that everyone decided was where a witch lived, and would dare each other to knock on the door, but never did. If I lived in a village now, which I don't, I'd probably be the witch.

I'm nine years old, walking along with my head slightly tilted to one side because I get a lot of ear infections now. I have to lie on my side parallel to the television, watching cartoons as Mum administers my ear drops. And we have a dog.

I began to read in the bathroom because it was the only room with a lock. If I was missing long enough, I would hear my mum call my name faintly from somewhere in the house. 'You've always been a thinker, haven't you?' she said once as she saw me coming out of the bathroom, book in hand.

Dad and I drove to the forest. It was cold even though

it was May. I had a small bag of dog treats in my hand, to entice the dog back on to its lead, when the walk was over, which made me wonder if the dog even liked us, as a family. One of the books I liked to read was about local ghosts and I would scare myself senseless. I remembered a story about a haunted wood somewhere in England that made people cry or have homicidal thoughts.

We walked all the way to the other side of the woods and perched on a fallen tree trunk, for a few moments, to take in the view. From here, we could see cows, farmhouses and the mountains beyond. Dad liked landscapes; he must have done because that's what he painted. But, mainly, he liked to paint them from memory. I think this was so he wouldn't have to worry about making mistakes or getting the colours right. Looking at his finished paintings, which he kept in the shed, I knew that mud wasn't really that orange or snow that blue, but it didn't matter to me or Dad. It mattered to people like Mrs Pugh, who humiliated me in primary school for painting a red sun, when all the other nine-year-olds had painted a yellow one. *Chill out, Miss – it's a painting, not a documentary*, I remember thinking as she took the painting from my stubby hand, telling me to start again. I decided from then on I would do the exact opposite of whatever Mrs Pugh told me. The incident made me mistrust primary colours. For many years, I had assumed these three colours were so called because these were often the only colours available to me, in primary school. I was one of the first children in my class to discover other shades, because Mrs Pugh had said not to mix the paints and make a mess, so I did.

Sometimes after school, before Dad got home from work, I would go to the shed and stand in front of his landscapes. It made me feel closer to him because they revealed something of his inner landscape to me. I could see what he had seen. I knew that Dad worked long hours, but I wasn't yet sure what he did. I knew that he had longed to be an actor or an artist, but that he wasn't either of those things.

We took the same path back through the woods, where the trees were at their most dense, letting in very little light. It was the scariest part. Dad was very tall and slender, with dark features. His face was gentle but contained a coldness, when looked at from certain angles. He would usually walk just ahead of me, hunched slightly, leaning forward almost. I became good at reading the back of his neck. I would know when he was in the mood for play and when I should be quiet. I became adept at navigating his moods. Like when a huge dog would appear and I would want to stand and admire it, but he would get stressed about our dog becoming frightened and would want to get home. Or his annoyance at my blackberry-stained fingers and clothes when we would go there in the summer and I would pick fruit.

On this particular walk, I remember his hairy hands on the gatepost as he helped me to climb over. I remember asking him if he had always liked painting. He told me a story about how, as a young man, he'd had various jobs, on building sites, in warehouses and in a framing shop, where he made the wooden frames by hand. He liked this job because he was, at least, making something. Most of the customers who came in, he said, just wanted their photographs or certificates framed, but occasionally someone would bring in a painting that would move him and he didn't know why. He started collecting posters of some of the Old Masters, which he'd send off for from the back of a magazine and would take three weeks to arrive.

'I would have loved to have framed a painting,' I recall him saying.

I loved that he became interested in art via their frames; this is like becoming interested in stand-up because you love microphones.

No child is ever entirely ten, they are always 'nearly eleven'. I knew what this rush was about. It was about needing to know more. I was convinced that there was some secret message contained in these woods for me, and that I just had to be patient. Some extra clue or detail about life that I didn't yet know, that hadn't been taught to me in school. Perhaps this would take the form of an enchanted deer appearing from behind a tree. The deer would lead me down a path. It would use an antler to make a tear in the universe, in space and time, and when I looked through the rip and saw what was there, the deer would grin and say, 'Do you understand?' and I would nod and say, 'Yes. I do.' Then with his other antler he would scrape all the old knowledge off my heart, before placing me back on the path where I had been, my esoteric education now complete.

Around about this time, of being nearly eleven, I was given a book about how the body worked. I had to stop reading it because of all the war imagery. Erections were described as 'little soldiers standing to attention', and advice was given on how to 'arm yourself' against the 'bloodshed' of periods.

When we walked past the fields where the cows always stood in groups, like mums, I asked my dad, 'Do cows have periods?'

'I think so,' he said.

'Do you have periods?' I asked.

'No,' he said. I was still confused and a little unsure as to what to expect when it finally happened. That night, I looked at my face in the bathroom mirror to see if I looked any different now that I knew about periods. I blew my nose and green snot came out and I wondered if this was a sign that my body was readying itself for this momentous event.

I went on a school trip to a city farm. My small village school was close to several working farms, so I'm not sure why we travelled into the city to see animals. For the other schoolkids the novelty was the animals; for us, it was the city element that was interesting.

On the way, our coach broke down outside an Ann Summers shop and the RE teacher had made us draw the curtains, so that we couldn't look. When we finally arrived, it was a huge disappointment. There was a goat tied to a post that had rolled in its own shit. Some of the girls started crying because they felt sorry for it. The boys kicked manure at one another. The woman who worked there swore more than anyone I had ever met. 'Get off, you cunt,' I heard her say in a harsh Cardiff accent, to a pig that had tried to bite her. It was the first time I had heard a woman use that word.

In the main barn, a cow sounded very distressed. By the time I ran over, two of the calf's legs were sticking out of the cow. The same woman, the 'cunt' woman, was tugging at the legs. We held our breath, getting ready for the big moment. The calf's head appeared with its eyes closed, trying to shake off the creamy stuff around its ears. Then, finally, the whole body burst out and landed with a thud. Everyone clapped as if it had been a party trick. The calf lay very still. 'Please open your eyes,' I said into my sleeve. When it finally did, the adults sort of laughed and the children said things like, 'Oh my God, I love her.' The birth had left me feeling strangely hungry, as if I also needed to eat for two. When I got home that night, my parents were eating ice cream in front of *Coronation Street*. When I told them what I'd witnessed, my dad shushed me, so I went into the kitchen and ate the sweetest, but quietest, thing I could find, so no one would know I was eating.

It's autumn and the paths are muddy. I'm fourteen and my trainers are too small now, but I won't let Mum buy me new ones because the 'worn' look is in trend.

We walked in silence for about ten minutes, the dog obediently by Dad's side on its lead. We paused by the stream so I could take a few deep breaths and Dad could get something out of his welly. The week before, the nice doctor had come to our house and told my mum that I had to start walking every day, so I didn't lose muscle. Purple-red spots had appeared on my body a few weeks beforehand and I was too tired to get out of bed. The diagnosis was something called purpura haemorrhagica. I remember Mum and I learning how to pronounce it, and thankfully I got better very quickly. The memory of having this illness only came back to me recently, and when I looked it up, curiously it said that it was most common in young animals, not people.

It's not that I wasn't paid attention to, but when I was ill I was the centre of attention, which was even nicer. Mum made me cakes.

Most of my information about my dad came from her. She knew all the details about his life. He could confide in her so effortlessly, it would seem, but why not me? It was like we were competing for his attention.

As Dad and I continued to take the dog to the forest, to help me get stronger, I began to wonder who he was. I knew he was an only child born in Pontypridd, but there was so much I didn't know, things like if he liked school or not, if he could swim, who his best friend was. The only thing I had was an impression that his childhood had been lonely, and I don't know why I thought that. Mum once told me in the kitchen when we were washing up that my father's earliest memory was of holding a slice of bara brith cake on a crocheted doily, standing in the front room of the terraced house he grew up in. I thought about that every time I ate a piece of bara brith. I don't even like the taste of it that much, but cake is cake.

Even though I was feeling much better, often on these walks I would find myself mute. I would simply stop talking, eat the sweets in my pocket that I had secretly put there, and stare down at the path as we walked. He didn't mind me being quiet, but he didn't ask why I was quiet, either. But how can you articulate anxiety at that age anyway? You can't.

I am conscious of my wide shoulders, so I try to pull them back when I walk. I hold my full stomach in. I am fifteen and binge-eating madly. My coat is too tight, which makes me feel like a stuffed glove. A wool scarf is wrapped around my mouth as I have just had my first filling and it hurts. The dog is full-sized now and strong.

This was the first time I had heard my dad use the word 'lover' and I detested it. In the centre of the wood was a small clearing, with flattened tree stumps ideal for resting.

'I'll never have another filling done,' I said, holding my cheek as I sat down, 'it's too painful.'

'You won't have to if you brush your teeth properly,' Dad said.

'I'm going to have them all removed! And wear false teeth, so I'll never have to have a filling again.'

'It won't be very romantic,' he said, 'when you're older and you have to lean across your lover and say, sorry, darling, I'm just going to take my teeth out, and put them in a glass of water by the bed.' I winced.

I had just come back from an exciting month in London doing the National Youth Theatre. I had never been to London before, and I was excited but intimidated by the idea of being there. I remember loving the snug little dorm room, when I first saw it, that was to be my home for the next month. The building was a large, grey brutalist structure in North London, with heavy doors that banged and woke me in the night. I made friends easily and increased my stamina for alcohol. But I also recall how I had been too scared and full to the brim with shame to use the communal shower room, just a short walk along the corridor from my room. I washed every morning using the small sink in the corner of my room, instead, but it was difficult. The sink was at an odd angle, and three weeks in, bits of my body began to itch. I was everything a young, budding actress should have been, except for the fact that I was laminated in cream and had hidden sweat rashes. I tried to ignore my skin and focus on the positives, like how ideal the tiny sink was for teeth brushing, so at least my teeth would be well looked after.

Occasionally, on these walks in the woods, Dad and I would look at each other for a moment. I suspect it was to do with how similar we were. It was a look that acknowledged our alikeness, our shared characteristics and the fact that we struggled in much the same way.

When the dog was out of sight, he said, 'Your mother said you made a lot of friends at Youth Theatre?'

'Yeah, it was fun,' I said in a downward inflection, hoping he would ask more questions, but he didn't.

There was always a lingering formality there. Isn't it strange to feel shy around your own father? It was hard for me to gauge how he truly felt about anything. When you don't really like yourself, life isn't about likes and dislikes, it's one long defence. Maybe that's why he didn't like to paint self-portraits.

Films were one of the few topics on which he had some confidence. Around about this time, he began sharing his love of cinema with me. We started with Kubrick, then Orson Welles, Visconti, Fellini, Hitchcock and others I don't remember. It was always male directors. To begin with, my taste was his taste, because that's how I knew to get love, by pleasing, navigating others' wants and needs.

When 9/11 happened, we had just come to the end of watching *Dr. Strangelove*, the screen was full of images of nuclear explosions, moments before we turned over to watch the news.

'I couldn't go on living if anything happened to your mother,' he warned me once, 'I would want to die.' This was late one night after he had shown me *Barry Lyndon*. *But what about me?* I thought. *What about me? I would still need you.*

His appreciation for the arts was handed down to me, as if I were the eldest son, receiving special knowledge. It was his way of reaching out to me. I inherited his passions, along with his depressive nature and insecurities.

I'm wandering through the trees in a dream-like state. My body is now hard all over apart from my padded bra. I'm tall and lean and twenty-two.

I had come home to visit my parents. We had taken the dog for a walk, because Mum had a migraine. I was only there for the weekend before I would go back to London again. I was living in East London now, in a house with some arty postgraduates. We had been broken into so many times in one year that we had started to leave cake out for the burglars. I smoked many rollies and wore so many black polo-neck tops that my neck always stayed much paler than my face.

This was my third attempt at life in London. All my previous attempts had failed after I had run out of money or got fired from another job and would return, broke, back to Wales. This was causing much concern for my parents.

The first job I had was on a beauty counter, where the intense perfumes gave me headaches. Daily visits from the cruelly named department manager, Tiffany Cobbledick – who, at her own insistence, we called Mrs Cobbledick rather than Tiffany – were the only moments of light relief. Worse still, after trying to jump from the back of a Routemaster bus I had landed on the road and acquired a perfect black eye. Mrs Cobbledick took one look at me and said I had to temporarily work 'in shoes', because I looked too ugly for beauty.

The path from the car park to where the woods began was very straight, as straight as the picture frames I imagined Dad had made, as a young man. I watched him stride ahead. I lingered, checking out my bruise in the car wing mirror. He stopped and turned to see where I was. He beckoned me to hurry up, so I jogged along the path to catch up with him. He walked quickly. I didn't like walking at that pace, but I didn't say anything. I was going through all that day's events to work out what I'd done wrong. I was wearing a long silk shirt with jeans. I'd had the shirt since I was sixteen, and it was as long as a dress, so that most of the material stuck out from the bottom of my short anorak. I'd only worn it because I didn't want to get mud on any of the clothes I had brought back with me from London. It had been scrunched up at the back of a wardrobe. The silk shirt looked too nice for the woods. I worried that the fanciness of the silk shirt was adding to his annoyance somehow.

A few metres from the gate, he said, 'You don't get night buses alone, late at night, do you?' I wanted to reply by saying, 'Why didn't you come to my graduation?' A question I hadn't been brave enough to ask yet. But instead I just said no – even though I did, nearly every night.

When we reached the rusty gate he stood on the dog's foot by accident and it yelped. He swore and then quickly said, 'You can't move back to London if you don't have a job there, can you?'

'I'll find one,' I said.

'It's not that easy,' he said.

'I've found loads of jobs,' I said, pulling the gate open. The bottom of the gate was stuck in mud and I wasn't strong enough to free it. 'You lived in London when you were young,' I said.

He moved me out of the way with his shoulder and started pulling the gate towards him. 'I'll do it,' he said.

'Anyway,' I suddenly said, 'I can't afford taxis, so I have to get a night bus sometimes, but it's totally fine.'

He didn't reply but continued to angrily tug at the gate. I suddenly felt a surge of annoyance at how selective his concern was. Why now this sudden fear of cities and me in them? Failure or not, this experience was rightfully mine. I put my hands back on the gate to help. 'Just let me do it,' he said. Mud flicked on to the hem of my silk shirt. I grabbed the metal bar one down from the top one and yanked it towards me. The rust pinched the skin of my hands. I let go.

'Your father's gone for a lie-down before *Coronation Street*,' Mum announced later that evening. She had made a bara brith loaf using my nan's recipe.

Coronation Street was on five times a week, and my parents never missed an episode. The storyline that night involved a character who had just come home from university. She was studying for an arts degree, as had I. You could always tell which characters were university students because they still went to the pub, just like everyone else, but they wore less make-up than the other women, and often wore a simple ponytail and a T-shirt. I felt at home with these char-acters, because they never seemed ashamed of their roots; if anything, they were a little apologetic for their exposure to culture.

My world began to change when I went off to university. My mind began to grow like the widening puddles in the woods.

I'm moving very slowly with my left arm in a sling. One foot slightly turning inwards with each step. It's dusk on a summer's evening in July. Quiet country lane.

My dad drove and I sat beside him reading, a piece of my mum's bara brith wrapped in tinfoil on my lap. The cake was as tough as metal. My parents had moved to mid-Wales and I had visited them for the night, just to see their new house. It was a nice cottage that slanted slightly and looked like it could withstand all weather. And now Dad was driving me back to the train station. We bickered about which radio station to put on in the car. I had accidentally pressed a button, which had caused the CD player to start playing a track by Moby. I remember wondering who in our family owned a Moby CD when it happened. Because I was looking down at my book, I had no warning, but suddenly there was an incredibly loud bang and we were spinning out of control. The car was turning so fast and I remember screaming and shouting 'Oh God, no' in absolute terror. The force was pinning me to my seat, the seat belt cutting into me, as we spun and spun. It felt like we spun for a long time, but it was probably seconds. Then we hit something else and there was another bang, which sent my body forward and up. And finally it stopped, everything was very still and quiet. *I'm dead*, was my first thought – *I have shown such promise and now I'm dead*. I looked down at my body, there was no blood. One shoe and my glasses had come off, and the bara brith was on the floor, still in one piece. I knew that we were in the middle of the dual carriageway and I worried that the car would get hit again. I looked over at my dad. He was slumped in his seat, not moving, eyes closed. *I'm not dead, but he is*, was my next thought. The car was full of white powder and I thought maybe it was smoke and that the car was going to explode, but I found out later that it had been from the airbags. I'd remembered from watching *Casualty* that you should keep repeating the injured person's first name, to keep them conscious, which is what I decided to do, rather than use 'Dad'. When the paramedics arrived, on hearing this, they asked if he was my partner and I remember feeling horrified. At least they didn't say 'lover'.

I didn't feel the immense pain until I was lying in the back of the ambulance, on a stretcher, and I didn't cry until I was in intensive care. I had to lie very still on my back, which created a dull ache at the back of my head. And the tears fell over my cheeks and on to the pillow, making it wet, because I couldn't wipe them away.

Eventually, a nurse massaged my hand open because it was so tense from holding on to my seat as the car spun round. The doctor told me that I was lucky to be alive and that the seat belt had saved my life, but it had also broken every bone in its path. My knee also felt like it had imploded. My father was in a different room. He had cracked his skull. As the doctor talked me through what had happened to my body, it reminded me of when I looked under my doll's skirt for the first time, as a child. It was like I was suddenly acutely aware of my own architecture, for the first time in my life. Until then, I had taken my body and everything it did for granted. When Mum got to the hospital, she was distraught. I asked her for the small hand mirror from her handbag, and when I looked into it the adrenaline had made my face look so young, and my pupils were the biggest I'd seen them since doing that MDMA in Thailand.

It was a huge relief when I could leave the hospital and be back in my own bed again. My English grandfather had come to see me. He asked me how I was feeling. 'About the same,' I said. Then he said, 'Well, at least now you'll lose some weight.' It's an interesting response to someone who has just nearly died. After he left I cried till my nose became clogged and that's when I rang B, and that's why she had wanted him dead, on my behalf.

The policeman in our living room, a week later, talked quietly, head to one side. I stared down at my sling. Another car had hit our car. Fifty miles an hour it was travelling. I remember seeing it written down on the police report. My dad simply hadn't seen the car. 'We believe it was a blind spot,' the policeman said helpfully. My mum clutched her chest, and offered them some cake. She had become the main carer for Dad and me, as we began healing, her hysteria showing up in her baking, which was how she coped.

'Is there anything else you're concerned about, or that you'd like to ask about?' the policeman said with a half-arsed smile. For a moment I considered telling him about how my periods had stopped, but decided not to. In truth, my lack of menstruation didn't concern me, it impressed me. It was as if my body was wise and couldn't be lied to. It reminded me of something I'd read, about how animals refuse to breed in captivity, sensing that the conditions are too traumatic to bring life into.

Dad was quiet. I didn't blame him for the accident. He was so self-critical, I worried about him. He had a way of pushing people away by disappearing into a rich and private inner life. I knew this because I recognised it in myself. Perhaps utterly irrelevant, or perhaps he was daydreaming slightly when the crash happened. Either way, he never drove again and neither have I.

The next few months passed by in a haze of opioids. The moment of impact was like being inside an explosion and I would replay the moment of impact, all the time. It woke up my body several times a night with a jolt of adrenaline. We were both lucky to survive. Everyone told me so.

Things were changed. Death was all around. It was there every time I breathed in and out as my broken sternum filled with pain. A near-death experience means you can't go back to denial. Death went from the abstract to the concrete in the moment of collision. Dad looked the same to the world, apart from the slight swelling on the side of his head, where it had hit the car frame.

We could only manage a short walk together, but we made it down to the lane and back. When we reached the house with the stone toads outside, he was out of breath and had to lean against a telegraph pole. 'I'm sorry,' he kept saying. But I didn't know if he meant sorry about not being able to walk any further or for driving the car that day.

Nearly a year later, I was ready to move back to London again. I could tell Dad wasn't quite the same. His shaken brain was slower and more confused. I first noticed the change when I looked at some of his drawings. They were less detailed, with less aliveness. It was the beginning of the end. But it was also the beginning of me figuring out how to ask for him. The crash had made me realise that there was an absence. The night before I left, I bravely asked him if we could find a way to be in touch more. He nodded enthusiastically.

Life in London was difficult to begin with. The first time I heard that same Moby track playing in an Urban Outfitters, I felt dizzy and had to leave. I hadn't anticipated how dependent my body had become on the strong pain-killers. After a few weeks, a postcard arrived for me. On the front was a picture of Brecon on a sunny day. It was from Dad. When I saw how sad and scribbly the handwriting was, how unconfident the spelling and grammar were, I instantly understood and could finally release the illusion that it had ever been about me. I saw his deep insecurity at having left school with very little to show for it. I felt the class war within himself, the inverted snobbery that gave him a love for all things learned, whilst never feeling good enough to join in.

Friends' fathers seemed to have the comfortable, confi-dent ease that middle-class dads have. I longed for him to have some of that, whatever it was. My father was happiest when he was holding a full pint in his hand, or was with others who had also escaped their past.

I bet the postcard had been my mother's idea and she probably posted it, but it didn't matter. It was the beginning of my dad and me addressing our neglected relationship.

I walk like I'm wearing an invisible heavy backpack (from wearing heavy backpacks all the time). I'm in my early thirties now. Dad and I walk slowly through some fields on our way back to the house. Dark Welsh skies above us.

He liked to tell me the names of the people he couldn't

remember any more, but I had to try to work out who he meant with just the descriptions and gestures. It was tiring.

This walk was part of our effort to connect. We talked about the accident, his childhood, the memory clinic where they would test cognitive decline by asking him questions like: who is the prime minister? And can you name twelve animals? I rubbed his arm. He was already showing early signs of dementia.

I could hear that his vocabulary was smaller. He was losing words. *Quick!* I would think. *No silences, we don't have time.* In an ideal world, this would have been ten years ago, when there was still time, but we are doing our best with the time we have left. Sometimes on these walks, I would think: *What if either one of us would be a disappointment to the other? What if there was no great mystery to him? What do I need to know?*

But there was something about being in nature that allowed us to talk freely. There was less oppressive context to grapple with, surrounded by nature. The beauty helped too, and maybe even the effect of large areas of one colour on the human brain. In cities, you don't see that. Where else does a person see that much green all at once, other than in nature?

I found out many things that day. He told me the story about when he was twenty-six, the age I was when the crash had happened. He had stood outside the Royal Academy of Dramatic Art, smoking a cigarette, watching the other hopeful auditionees walk up to the imposing stone building. He had been given a recall but was too scared to go in, so he'd gone to find a pub instead. He had spent his last bit of money on drink and couldn't afford the train fare back home to Wales, so had spent the night on a park bench. The next morning a stranger took pity on him and gifted him the train fare home to Pontypridd. He told me he had wanted to be an actor from a young age but was too embarrassed to tell anyone. A building site in Pontypridd back then wasn't the sort of liberal atmosphere where you could admit to such things. So he kept his interests hidden. He once remarked that he worried that 'acting wasn't a job for men'. He talked about his father's hands, calloused from years of labour. And his mother's hands too, how we'd all heard her say, when she was alive, 'I've worn away my fingerprints from scrubbing so many steps.'

A wonderful paradox occurred. In the forgetting, he had remembered something: the bara brith. He remembered that he had forgotten something in the scene. For a long time, he thought the memory was banal, but then he realised that there was something missing from the memory: his father lying in an open casket. Someone is stroking his hair and telling him that he can go and kiss his father goodbye on the cheek, if he wants to. This is what had happened just before someone passed him the piece of cake.

He learnt things about me too.

When I told people how much closer I felt to him, after we had shared our real feelings with one another, I said it as if I had discovered this new thing. But friends looked at me like I had just said something so obvious, confused as to how I didn't already know that. It made me think of the time a friend had said to me very earnestly, 'Pasta tastes so much nicer with sauce,' or when another friend had said, 'Make-up goes on so much easier if you put a bit of moisturiser on first.' Everyone else knew these were obvious things.

I used to think that intimacy was about saying everything that had ever happened to you at someone, and then they sort of *had to* care about you. It hadn't occurred to me that relationships were about two people being vulnerable.

I'm tired, heavy and tense. I walk in sensible shoes, occasionally pausing to sigh and rub my neck.

I was trying to fall asleep downstairs on the sofa bed in my parents' house in mid-Wales. All day Mum had kept telling me how grateful she was that I was there and that she knew I was very busy. I kept saying I wanted to be there. Their house was so cold, especially at night, and I never knew why I was the only one who felt it. At around two or three in the morning, Dad walked into the living room, in just his pyjama bottoms, and stood still at the end of the bed and murmured, 'I don't know where I am. It's all dark. I don't know where I am. Where am I then?'

I gently took him by the arm and steered him back to his bedroom. The following day he lit one of the gas stove rings, filled the plastic kettle with water and then placed it on the stove to boil. Thankfully it triggered the smoke alarm pretty quickly. I rushed in and found Dad sat at the kitchen table in his dressing gown, looking almost sheepish. I put the fire out and threw the melting kettle out the back door. Later, when Mum was washing up, I explained to her what had happened and she sort of chuckled. The kitchen still smelt like chemicals and fire.

A few days later, social services paid them a visit and said that they weren't coping. Looking after another person's body is hard. Mum had cared for him for so long and now she was ill. This was the price of love, according to her.

The first few times I went to visit him at the home, he would leap up and say, 'Right! This way.' Then he'd walk and walk up and down the corridors, whistling, as if he were still at work. The long antiseptic-smelling corridors were not unlike those of the building where Dad had worked for many years. He would move quickly, opening doors he wasn't supposed to and tapping the walls with interest. I don't know how many miles he must have covered in a day. We all embraced the work story, it was easier than the truth. I brought him his heavy bunch of keys, hoping that, when he clutched them, time would feel less rubbed out. This rummaging and searching, I learnt, was quite universal amongst dementia sufferers, as a form of self-soothing. His words were nonsensical by now, but he still wanted to chat to the staff, as we passed, hoping to make a connection. This person speaks with the same cadence as my dad, but the words are incomprehensible. When it was time to go, he would agree and say that he'd 'best get on, anyway', and we would take on the deception, agreeing that he was busy and we were in the way. Sometimes he would just walk on the spot, like a character in a paused computer game. The nurses would gently encourage him into an armchair, where we'd have tea and cake. This was the only bit of normalcy we had left. Without language, we had to say everything that was needed with our eyes and hands. My hands often knew how I was feeling before I did.

They sometimes played old Westerns in the all-male dementia ward. My father was moved there after he tried to attack one of the nurses during the night, by grabbing her throat in a fit of psychosis. He had thought she was trying to kill him. It wasn't his fault of course, it was the disease, but I was crushed. In the day room of the men's ward, newly sedated, he would sit motionless in an armchair. The chairs were all arranged to face the large television in the corner. When he would nod off, his head drooped almost to the bellybutton.

He had lost the ability to draw, but he enjoyed cutting up old Christmas cards to make a collage, the first winter he was there, 'Silent Night' playing softly in the background, the pain of which was almost too piercing to listen to. I couldn't bear to think of him deprived of his creativity.

I'm walking alone.

When I arrived, he didn't look alive any more. Each person had their own stopping point for wanting to visit him, which was understandable. It was too hard to bear, seeing him in this state of decay. The ward was a frightening and unpredictable place sometimes. It's hard to imagine any sort of limit being reached when it's someone you love, but then nothing about death had been how I imagined. During one of my last visits to the ward, I didn't recognise him and walked straight past. Anticipatory grief is a prison. Even though the separation had begun years before . . .

I watched as my father slowly lost his mind. The light behind his eyes began to fade, like a great fire was dying out. The memories fell, one by one. Many evenings, I sat next to his bed in the dementia ward, holding his hand, wondering if he was losing those memories in the reverse order of when they were made, so that one day only his first recollections would remain. If so, what would they be?

Before I left that night, when everyone else had left the room, he opened his eyes for a brief moment and looked at me. It was a look of happiness and calm because he had seen me, one last time. He closed his eyes and went back to breathing quietly.

You think you're prepared, you're never prepared.

So that's what it feels like to be told a parent has died, I thought, when the nurse rang.

'He passed away ten minutes ago,' she said. At first, this was the detail that haunted me the most. He had just, just been alive. We were all gathered in the kitchen, waiting for the call. I couldn't remember exactly what I had been doing or thinking ten minutes ago, and that was the moment. The pain is so exquisite that I cannot believe it's possible.

At the funeral, my eulogy exposed his secret; I spoke of his hidden interests, his sensitivity, beauty and intelligence. Even though the separation had begun years before, I felt that we got our time together. I wished I had asked him more questions about his life and who he was but I was too shy to. Not everyone gets the time they need. The celebrant made some really awful and totally misjudged sexist jokes, but the resulting anger was actually quite a nice distraction from the pain of the day.

When we left the crematorium, it was snowing heavily, landing on our dark clothes.

I kept his favourite tie, his flat cap, his driving licence and a jug that he had made in art class when he was thirteen. His paintings are the only thing I own that have any real value or meaning to me. Today, two pictures of his hang, side by side, in my home. The landscapes depict the woods where we would walk. The colours and tones speak of his mood on that day. Whenever I feel that I don't know him directly, I can go to these pictures and see what he saw, all those years ago. People comment on the frames as much as they do the paintings.

13

MOONCAKE,
OR,
THE DISAPPOINTMENTS OF FAME

My father met famous people all the time, because he worked backstage in a large concert hall. 'The Dalai Lama? Oh yes. Very small, laughed a lot. Diana? Oh yes. Very tall, big nose. You were there when I met Nureyev? Don't you remember? You were very young. He gave you a rose.'

Maybe that's why I've never been that excited by the idea of fame. If you went to every single house in the British Isles and shook everyone's hand and said hello and maintained eye contact, for at least a minute, then you would be known to everyone, and technically famous. No one would judge you for having acquired fame so easily.

When the Chinese State Circus were performing a show at the concert hall, I was allowed to sit in the lighting box with a Coke and crisps and press the button when someone said, 'Now.' The button bathed the whole stage in red light. After the show, one of the performers gifted me an ornate paper fan and something sweet that looked like a large glazed bean, in a paper bag. On the way home I dropped the cake and chased it as it rolled and tumbled down a hill. It got run over by a van.

My parents were my original audience. Sometimes I was theirs.

But, if we are to get anywhere in this world, we must, at some point, learn to sever the ties between applause and self-worth.

14

OATCAKES

When you are sad, and the sadness is bottomless, you will do what it takes to escape yourself. If it meant using my savings to not be me, then that was a bargain. And it was under these conditions that I decided to get a personal trainer.

The 'payout' I had received from the car accident was the most money I had ever owned, through trauma and in general. This insurance money had no effect on the injuries themselves, but could at least act as a homage to the whole 'terrible experience'. And I enjoyed using this new word, 'payout'. 'Yeah, so, basically, I got a payout, in the end.' It had the stench of success about it, a certain matureness. My bones had successfully knitted back together, and I was told I was lucky to be alive. I moved a little awkwardly, but apart from that you couldn't tell that I had been through 'a terrible experience', or, at least, that's what I thought. I no longer counted the months since it had happened, but was still aware of the number, which was ten. Well, I guess that was all that dealt with, then.

When you first notice that you are depressed and maybe have been for a while, it seems almost amusing that you could have ever thought otherwise. That's what the illness does. Others knew I was depressed before me, as if I had been denying my fluency in a particular language, before leaving messages in the sky, in that same tongue.

One cold evening, I 'came round' to discover that I had been lying on my side, on the futon, for a long time, staring at a wall, more specifically, at a piece of White Tack that had been squished flat against it, at eye level, a thumbprint just visible. I was looking at it, wishing it was me, thinking how much easier existence would be if I was that small blob. I stared for so long that I felt my consciousness leave my own body and move a couple of inches towards the White Tack. For a few moments, 'I' only existed in the space between my body and that piece of adhesive. That's when I decided to google the phrase 'personal trainers in my area'.

From here on in, for the rest of this chapter, anything underlined is a lie and anything in italics is true but I didn't actually write, and the rest is an exaggeration, based on true events. I wasn't well at the time, and we should all bear that in mind. This is the story of why I lied to a personal trainer.

Dear Strawberry,

Just an email to follow up on your enquiry about
The Anthony Canada Method and The Anthony
Canada 10 Week 'Better You' Programme. The
Anthony Canada 10 Week 'Better You' Programme
does exactly what it says on the tin. We offer ten
weeks of one-to-one personal training sessions.
All the personal training sessions take place in
our specifically designed Anthony Canada Method
gym, which is in over two locations. Anthony and I
both offer PT (personal training) and we will divide
the PTSs (personal training sessions) between us,
depending on what your personal needs are. <u>There's
nothing we love more than seeing people thrive at
our studios</u>. I would welcome the opportunity to
work with you in achieving your fitness goals.

Look forward to hearing from you.

Just a quick question regarding the attached form.
Where it says 'What are your fitness goals?' you just
wrote 'no', I wondered if that was a mistake . . .

Be You, Be a Better You.

Becki Sommersville
Fitness Coach

PS Is this the right email address? Do you prefer to
be called Katy or Strawberry?

Dear Becki,

Thanks for getting back to me so quickly, and on Christmas Eve too! So nice.

Sorry for the confusion, it is Katy, yes, the email address is a different name to mine, and looks like I might be called Strawberry, but I'm not. *I use this email for junk and stuff I don't want to do.*

I don't have specific fitness goals, no, other than being able to wash my hair in the shower without my arms getting tired, but really it's more about managing mental health and feeling strong and just generally fitter, I think.

Can I just pay for one session to begin with, to see how I get on?

Thanks

Katy

PS I was in a terrible car accident but I'm OK now.

Dear Katie,

Sorry to hear about your mental problems. I completely understand.

My name and email address are one and the same, so at least we'll have no problems there!

There is an initial consultation fee, but then unfortunately, you will have to pay for all ten training sessions up front.

<u>This is truly a training programme like no other</u> because of Anthony Canada's <u>unique</u> approach to fitness, which involves exercising and health. FYI, Anthony began his fitness journey when he was a young guy, having to defend himself from teachers and pupils at school. He then built his first gym, from scratch, over nine years ago and since then we have gone (literally) from strength to strength. The Anthony Canada Method is a complete exercise and nutrition plan inspired by Anthony's martial arts training, whilst abroad and on holiday in the UK. We can adapt any of the exercises to suit your ability if you have limited movement due to your accident.

<u>Every great journey starts with one email</u> and we'll have you beach-body ready before you can say drop down and give me plenty!

Be You, Be a Better You.

Becki Sommersville
Fitness Coach

PS Is this the right email address for you?

Dear Becki,

Thanks, that's great. This is the right email address for me, yes *because obviously I'm replying, but if you mean 'best fit for my personality' then no.*

I've never met anyone who has built a gym from scratch, that's really impressive.

I'm not sure if I would say my movement is limited, it's certainly not unlimited. Post car crash, I find I can't swim very far without crying angry hot tears – something to do with muscle memory and trapped trauma, I'm assuming, but no GP will back me on this. I think I'm OK to take part in exercise. It might be good to start with something quite gentle though, adopting a sort of 'no pain, no pain' motto.

I don't have any plans to go to the beach, but OK, sounds great. *I don't know about 'beach-body ready', I'm certainly grateful to have a healthy, healed body. Besides, we evolved from the sea, so I think my body is more than 'ready'; if anything, it's overqualified.*

Thanks

Katy

Dear Katy,

Given that January & February can get very booked up. Please confirm your intention to proceed & if any of these dates suit you to ensure that these slots do not get booked up by others.

Available times:

6:30 a.m.: Wednesdays & Thursdays (& possibly Fridays and Mondays)

12 p.m. Wednesdays (& possibly Mondays)

Be You, Be a Better You.

Becki Sommersville
Fitness Coach

Hi Becki,

Yes, of course. I have to work on Wednesdays, so can I go for the 6:30 a.m. session on Monday? Do I need to bring anything, or will it just be sitting down? *And will Anthony Canada be there too, or will his presence remain simply titular?*

Be Me, Be a Better Me.

Katy

Dear Katy,

We will do a full assessment of your health, lifestyle and a fitness test.
And don't forget the clocks go back, so it will feel like 5:30.

Be You, Be a Better You.

Becki Sommersville
Fitness Coach

Becki,

I'm so sorry I didn't make it today. I must have written it down as Tuesday, not Monday, how silly! *I knew it was today, but I haven't lived in London that long and I still find it quite difficult to assess how long journeys will take, and I still, occasionally, get lost on the Underground. Becki, I'm tired. When I agreed to the appointment, I was trying to be kind to my future self, by imagining her as someone who was good at early starts, but future me didn't deliver, I'm sorry. That's why I didn't come.*

Be Me, Be a Better Me.

Katy

Hi Katy,

No problem at all.
    Ant and I can fit you in tomorrow?

Becki

Hi,

Yes, great. *I thought you'd be more cross.*

Thanks and sorry again.

K

Dear Katy,

Great first session today, Katy. And lovely to meet you. I just caught up with Anthony, and he said to say sorry that he couldn't be there, apparently someone had 'a panic attack' on the Tube, and it made him late.

I completely respect you not wanting to be weighed because of your 'political reasons'. We'll just focus on fitness, rather than on weight loss, as you say, yes – a woman can want to do exercise for other reasons than just weight loss, I agree with you, that people need love at every size and that shame never worked as a method to change anyone, ever. I think that's a really interesting idea.

I've included your nutritional plan for the next ten weeks, with a few personal tips from me, which I've written in the margins (for example, I find that oatcakes make a great substitute for things like bread and cake, and Parma ham is a great alternative to cereal) and whey has no flavour so it's really versatile.

Don't worry about the mirror tile in the toilet, it's always been loose.

Becki Sommersville

PS Sorry quick q: did you leave an iPod on top of the bin?

Hi Becki,

No, It's not mine. I got one for Christmas, but it was stolen as soon as I came back to London. It's the third break-in we've had. The landlord doesn't care.

What's whey?

See you on Thursday.

BM, BABM

Katy

PS Was that Anthony and his wife on the front of all those fitness magazines in the rack on the wall? When you were searching for a pen, I had a quick flick through, but it didn't say who they were. *The articles all seemed a little repetitive, like exercise I suppose. There was something about the way the oiled man and woman, on the front, were each holding the ends of that big twisted rope that made me think they were partners, like they'd been holding a rope for a long time. And their matching yellow outfits of course.*

Hi Katy,

Really good second training session today. Hope you enjoyed. Your arms are quite long and your wrists are almost too small for your body, so I think push-ups will always be challenging for you.

Did you get a chance to speak to your boss about getting a standing desk in your office, as I suggested?

Whey is a sort of protein. It's basically the stuff that is left if you press down on milk.

Ant is going to join us on Thursday (yay!) to do some martial arts training. You should see him in action, he's awesome!

Becki

Hi Becki,

Aren't my wrists supposed to be smaller than my body?

I'm not allowed a standing desk.

I've never pressed down on milk.
See you then.
<u>Sorry about being late today for our session.</u>

Katy

Hi Katy,

Great session today K.

I'm sorry to hear that you have had no luck with the standing desk. Your poor posture is probably because your desk isn't ergonomically set up at your office, so you could speak to someone about that. Also, cold draughts from air conditioners or an open window can cause neck muscles to tighten, so watch out for that.

Try and do those buttock exercises this week, as I demonstrated, before our next session on Monday.

Becki Sommersville

Thanks Becki,

I didn't know that. I do get a sore neck sometimes. It might be because I sleep on a futon.

Thanks

Katy

Hi Katy,

It shouldn't be a problem, as long as it's a relatively new mattress . . .

Thanks

B

Hi Becks

It's very old.

Thanks.

I have to unfurl it each night (and roll it up each morning), because my room is very small. Is there anything more depressing than coming home, exhausted, knowing that at some point, you'll have to unfurl a futon? I start thinking about it from about 6 p.m. onwards every night. It's very distracting for me, very hard to concentrate on what people are saying to me post six o'clock, knowing that I'll have to unfurl a futon later that evening. That's how I knew the house had been broken into: the muddy footprints travelling diagonally across my futon. My bedroom is on the ground floor. It was the one time I had unfurled it before going out that evening. The intruder came back again a few months later, but there was nothing worth taking. I didn't sleep for two nights after the second break-in. Every noise woke me, I tried to be brave about it, but I think it's totally normal to worry if you think you're in danger, don't you, Becki? The third time, my housemate and I had just arrived home, when a man burst out of the front door and pushed past us, my housemate's laptop was under his arm. 'My play!' my housemate exclaimed, as if the power of art could make him reconsider, as if he might pause, and say, 'What's it about?' before making his decision to steal it or not. It wouldn't have ended well anyway, because whenever someone asked her what one of her plays was 'about' she would say, 'Sorry, do you mean what happens, or what's it about?' and the conversation always ended after that. The burglar and the play ran off into a nearby graveyard. We chased him for a bit, until we got scared and out of breath (we were both binge-smokers back then).

After the police had seen the footprints, I furled the futon back up and slept in my housemate's bed, rather than be alone. We all know from podcasts now that the world becomes dangerous for women, when alone.

Thanks Becki, see you Monday.

Katy

Hi K,

<u>Well done for today's session</u>. Don't worry if you can't do all the exercises yet, we can build up your stamina. I'm sorry to hear that you hate exercise and that it makes you feel 'blank', but you did really well today. I hadn't thought about that before, but I

suppose a place full of mirrors and bright lights can be 'a bit of a downer'.

I should have mentioned that I'm quite hands on with my approach, I didn't mean to startle you.

Anthony apologises for not being there today, but he ripped his Thailand trousers, so he had to go to mine to change.

Hope you had a good day at the office.

Becks

Hi Becki,

God, your emails are boring. I'm sorry, Becks. I take it back. That was unfair of me. I woke up in a bad mood because the landlord still hasn't done anything about the damp patch in the corner of my room.

Why does Ant keep spare trousers at your place?

Sorry that I was late again today for our session.

My boss is called Christine Moorhead. I'm too scared to ask her for a standing desk, but I will mention about the air con and make sure that I'm not near any draughts or windows from now on. It's a small office – only four of us – but I'll let you know if I make any progress.

'There are as many muscles in the buttocks as there are parts to an egg' is my new favourite fact. I had no idea that a strong bum was the basis for good back health.

<u>I enjoyed today's session.</u>

On the whole, I do detest exercise, but not with you, strangely. When I did those bum exercises correctly, you seemed so happy, and I appreciated that. I'm glad you mentioned your hands. Sometimes, when I'm not expecting the touch, I'm prone to flinching. I'm thinking of when a boss of mine once touched the small of my back and I dropped something, or the time the man swimming behind me grabbed my ankle to signal that he wanted to overtake me, or the time a producer groped me onstage but in such a way that the audience couldn't see, or the time the teacher adjusted my body in a yoga class and there was a feeling of wrongness about it.

But, no, I don't mind you being hands on. It's nice that you're so supportive, but it's almost as if you're doing most of the work, like you get carried away. At one point, I think you were taking all the weight of the weight when I was supposed to be lifting the weight and I couldn't feel any strain at all, I wasn't really doing anything. It was nice for me, obviously, but I worry that I won't make any progress if we continue in this vein. Whilst it is inspiring to feel oneself in the presence of, in terms of exercising, a talent greater than one's own, I hope you're not unconsciously, of course, enabling my feebleness. I hope you're not keeping me weak deliberately, like a cruel mother, so that I will need you (and pay you) more.

It can't be easy working in your industry. Because manu-facturing employment has declined drastically, and the service sector has grown so much, there are lots of jobs like personal trainer now, I suppose. Whilst the human services market must be a fast-growing area, I imagine it's a competitive field. A hundred years ago, Anthony might have been utilising those big muscles of his to make a drystone wall and now he lifts ropes! Funny, isn't it?

Katy

Hi Kate,

That's great to hear.

Even though this was only our third training session together, hopefully you feel as though you are making progress.

Are you managing to eat oatcakes at 4 p.m. instead of snacking from the vending machine that you said was installed recently in your office?

B

Hi Bex,

I've got everyone in the office hooked on oatcakes now. The vending machines are practically derelict. At 4 p.m., a woman named Sandra passes by my desk and usually she says, 'Do you want anything from the vending machine?' and I say, 'Surprise me,' but now she doesn't even bother to ask. But at 4 p.m. today I glanced over at Sandra and she was eating oatcakes, laughing at something on her computer, with her shoes off. She looked really happy. Christine Moorhead is leaving too, and it's all thanks to oatcakes.

Thanks

Katy

PS I had a dream about Ant last night, even though I've never met him, but I know what he looks like from the photos on all the gym walls. Why are there none of you?

In the dream, we were sat in a horrible bar, late at night. He was gloating about his naturally fast metabolism, over drinks, when he said that he had married someone he shouldn't have married. We went back to his and had sex in his kitchen. He made a protein shake the second after he came. The dream took me by surprise, because he's not my type at all. Apparently, if you dream of having sex with someone in a dream, it actually means that you want something they have . . . his thick wrists maybe?

Hi Katy,

Your office sounds like a really fun place to work. Great that you're enjoying the switch to oatcakes. You mentioned that it's your birthday coming up. Birthday cake isn't on the nutritional plan, sorry.

Lol! You could always have a couple of extra oatcakes instead. They do ones with cheese and chives in.

Looking forward to seeing you.

Becki

PS Anthony won't be joining us tomorrow – he knocked down an entire family when he was out running. That man doesn't even know his own strength! There's a lot of paperwork basically. He might not have time to join us now.

Hi Becki,

OK, see you tomorrow.
I think it's good to eat birthday cake on your birthday though.
Damp patch is getting bigger. Hope it's not an omen.

K

Lol

See you tmrw

Becki

Hi Katy,

Great session earlier. We all have our off days, don't worry. Hopefully, you feel as though you are making progress in your fitness journey now? Speaking of which, even though we have only had four sessions, out of the ten you have paid for, do you want to extend to a further ten training sessions, so that we can carry on our <u>good</u> work together?

Sorry about the double-booking confusion earlier which meant we had to share the space with Ant and his client. Apparently, Ant did tell me that he had booked the gym, <u>but I must have forgotten</u>. But at least you got to see him in action, even if you didn't actually meet him properly.

Becki

Hi Katy,

Just checking you got my last email. Are we still on for our session tomorrow?

Thanks

Becki

Hi Becki,

I'm really sorry but I can't come to any more training sessions. I enjoyed our work together and I think you're a really good personal trainer. The thing is, I'm an alcoholic. I know that you don't do refunds, but, given the nature of the situation, I was wondering if you might make an exception. Sorry, if this email was a little intense. I'm not really OK and I need to sort it out, I think.

Katy

(Becki replies straight away, but I don't read it.)

Dear Katy,

I know it's been a few weeks, but I was just checking to see if you got my last email about no refunds.

Also, I saw you acting on telly last night! I'm a bit confused. So you don't work in an office?

Becki Sommersville
Fitness Coach

Dear Becki,

Sorry for not replying sooner.

I don't work in an office, no, so sorry.

I'll try to explain.

As a child, I was furious if someone took a photo of me seconds before I was ready or caught sight of a drawing before it was done. I've carried this perfectionism into my adult life. There's a long list of things I never did or allowed to happen, all because I wasn't ready. I always thought I needed to change first, before living. I confused longing with living. I've missed out on things I care about, all because I didn't feel ready to share myself. It was all a defence against intimacy, a very effective one, because it was lonely.

That first morning we met, it was easier to lie than to share myself. I didn't have the maturity to take part in any sort of conversational intimacy with you, especially so early in the morning, so I said I worked in an office. I thought there would be no follow-up questions if I said that. I didn't want you to know about my broken heart, my broken bones, but I didn't want you to know about my successes either. That is partly why I lied to you, Becki. My other fear was that you wouldn't believe me if I said I was on TV, because I wasn't attractive enough and didn't have the sort of body that would be chosen to be on TV. Plus, I didn't seem to take much pride in my appearance, as you might expect from a TV body: my leggings have holes in, because I still dress like I did in sixth form, because that's when I was happy. It is confusing, Becki, I agree. I can afford new leggings and I am on TV, you're right, I'm sorry. It was only a small acting job though, and it didn't pay that well, so I did really need the refund, so I could keep living in my small, damp, overpriced room.

In the months since I got your email, I have imagined you googling me, finding my name in the comedy listings, before turning up at a gig to confront me. A few nights ago, I was performing at a sketch night in Clapham and I thought I saw you. A woman was sat, alone, with her back to me. She had the same short blonde hair as you, the same athletic shoulders. The table was reserved for five. I hid. Five? You, Ant and some of the other trainers? Ant's wife and some rope? I sat on an old sofa backstage, imagining the five of you, now sat in your seats, gym clothes still on, Ant in a shirt maybe. The chant would begin as soon as I set foot on stage, 'LIAR. LIAR. LIAR. She's a LIAR.' The guy who ran the night would be livid, the audience confused. Ant would knock the mic out of my hand with a roundhouse kick, then the two of you would embrace. I wasn't even being paid to do this gig.

Becki, it wasn't you. This woman had long purple nails, which you'd never have.

Overwhelmed by the job of having to say what my job was, I lied, I'm sorry. It wasn't a complete lie, I have worked in offices. No one ever ate oatcakes though.

I once worked for a company that made bespoke ballet

supplies for children and dance students. Mainly I sat at a desk opening emails. Sometimes I would have to go into a small warehouse and find the items on tall wooden shelves, before packaging them up to be mailed. That was my favourite part of the job, because at least I was reaching people. There was also a shop in a separate building that sold dance paraphernalia. I was a big fan of tops with cut-out shoulders back then, which really seemed to excite one of the managers. He liked to come up behind my swivel chair and place a hand on each exposed bit of shoulder flesh and ask how I was getting on. But mainly I was left alone and at lunchtime would read the books on the shelves: biographies of dancers, dance history, nutrition for dancers. All contained picture after picture of beautiful female dancers. The books about nutrition said that dancers were athletes and therefore needed to eat for fuel and strength. This seemed like a beautiful lie to me, to imply that many dancers didn't go hungry. The only professional dancers I had ever known were all open about choosing cigarettes over food and choosing hunger over food. This honesty made my life more bearable.

Starving was a worthy cause if it meant looking that beautiful (something I no longer believe).

There were three young ballet students who regularly came into the shop together and smelt faintly of vanilla. I only heard bits of their conversations, but I knew they were involved in some sort of pact of deprivation. I heard them talk with pride, competition even, about how little they ate. 'I don't like drinking water, it makes my stomach stick out,' one of them said, calmly, as they each swallowed a few digestive enzymes out of a bottle, when they thought no one was looking. The girl who said she didn't like drinking water swallowed hers without water. On the way home, I googled digestive enzymes, I couldn't really tell what they did, but they were made from the pancreas of pigs.

I looked forward to them coming in, I felt drawn to them, perhaps I even fetishised their pain a little, I don't know.

One afternoon, I was sat at my desk alone when I had this vague sense of excitement and feeling of suspense, but didn't know why. A few moments later, someone came in from one of the other offices with an order and on their way out said, 'Oh, by the way, Sharon Stone's son is in the shop buying shoes.' So that's what the strange feeling had been: Sharon Stone. I snuck into the back of the shop and stood in the corner, partially hidden by a tall yucca. I wanted to see how beautiful Sharon Stone was, as if she needed to prove it to me. I wanted to see what type of beauty it was, with my own eyes, so that I could appreciate its value. Me and another girl from Wales took it in turns to deal with customers. Today had been her turn. I watched as she nervously placed the first ballet shoe on the son's foot. A man dressed like a bodyguard was stood next to them. Sharon was nowhere to be seen. I don't remember the child except that he had beautiful little feet. Everyone treated those little boy's feet with *extreme care and respect, as you would a very delicate clay.*

After our last session together, Becki, when you got me to walk on an incline, on that treadmill, for ages, I waited for the endorphin rush, but it never came. That night, I unfurled my futon, as per, and waited for the endorphin rush, but I remained numb. I wasn't sure I even existed if it hadn't been for my slight reflection in the iPhone screen. I felt alone, ashamed of feeling alone and ashamed of my own melodrama. I cried into the fattest part of the mattress until I fell asleep. At around three in the morning, the damp patch gave way and a whole section of ceiling landed with a frightening thud, not far from my head. I didn't even move. I didn't care.

I'm sorry, Becki, I just panicked and said I was an alcoholic, precisely because I'm not. Retrospectively speaking, perhaps I was trying to transmit to you my impulse for self-destruction, without actually having to confess anything, but mainly I hoped you would feel sorry for me and give me the money back.

There's something else, Becki. It troubled me when you made that comment about not eating cake on my birthday.

I turned twenty-one in an Italian restaurant in the West Midlands with a small group of friends. We drank so much acidic white wine that we couldn't even taste the food. The cake had arrived that morning by special delivery, bearing a '21' in light-blue icing. It was too babyish-looking for a twenty-one-year-old. I had carried it in its white cardboard box to the restaurant and placed it on a chair beside me, barely looking at it, embarrassed by its fussiness. At the end of the meal, I put the box in the centre of the table and opened the lid, but no one really wanted any. We all ignored the cake. The cake looked too aggressively happy. I don't think anyone ate much cake back then, or anything else. I closed the lid again. My parents had tried to reach out to me via cake, and it had failed. I was angry at their misplaced effort, their misdirected concern.

As we left, the waiters sort of lined up in front of the door and insisted on kissing us all on both cheeks. The oldest waiter said to me, 'Your face isn't beautiful but it's very honest,' as if he were rescuing me from a life of expecting too much. This sort of uninvited commentary was all the rage back then and we didn't even think to get angry, we simply tried to ignore it.

I walked home, hungry, from the restaurant back to my student accommodation, still holding the cake in its box. Out of sight and in my room, I opened the lid and, too scared to confront my real feelings or real emotional hungers, I began to eat and eat and eat. Sugar was something my body could trust, a reliable, dependable source of comfort. It's impossible to feel anything mid-binge and that's the point. But the sweetness is swiftly followed by something distinctly unsweet. Straight after the binge come the guilt and the self-loathing. I threw what was left of the cake in the bin. But I wasn't done.

A few moments later, I took it back out of the bin and continued to eat. Afterwards, I ripped the box up into small pieces and threw them away, so that in the morning no trace of the cake could be found. I hated myself for not being able to treat food normally, like other people did.

As I write this, I can't even remember how the cake tasted.

I'm 'cured', but it took about eight years of therapy and the cultivation of a small feminist library, and it's an ongoing process. Your nutritional plan was almost entirely devoted to oatcakes and eggs, like the diet of an athlete or an old person. But, either way, I knew that weeks of restriction and denial on your proposed regime would be dangerous for me, setting me up for more binging and feelings of being out of control again around food. I actually really like oatcakes, but I knew my therapist would go nuts if I didn't have cake on my birthday (if I had wanted to have cake). Once I broke the cycle of deprivation and overeating, all I wanted were the foods from my childhood that I wasn't supposed to eat, namely cake. That's why I wanted to eat birthday cake this year on my birthday and not an oatcake.

I wanted to eat cake because I can and I'm allowed and no one is going to tell me otherwise.

The problem with exercise is that you have to keep doing it. It's not a one-time thing, like chickenpox or drowning.

Somewhere I absorbed this notion that optimists

were uninteresting and that people who exercised were humourless. I'm not sure when my prejudice began. I don't even buy tampons if they have sporty packaging. Maybe I'm just jealous. It wasn't until I stumbled across the concept of 'sadness as an act of resistance' and the 'power of sadness' in Audrey Wollen's writing that I had an understanding of why I hadn't wanted my suffering to be jogged out of me. The unhappiness was perhaps trying to tell me something. It was useful.

It was only when I found out that Alanis Morissette did triathlons that I started to wonder if I had been the one in the wrong all along when it came to exercise.

As an undergraduate, I had made friends with women who were brilliant and powerful, passionately intelligent and funny. They seemed rebellious and impossibly glamorous, with their menthol cigarettes, asymmetrical haircuts and book recommendations. And yet I recall how it was the men who mainly spoke in lectures. The women were all quiet, at first, whilst the men spoke freely, like a mid- to late-noughties panel show. We were still trying to understand our power.

I apologise for this prejudice, Becki. I'm sure you do have a sense of humour. You treated my body as kindly as Sharon Stone's son's feet were treated. There was something maternal about your instruction, which made me want to both hug you and push you away. You have left me with the desire to exercise, though I don't actually do any, but this is progress (don't you think?) so it hasn't been a complete waste of time.

I once had a body that was strong. After the crash, a doctor came to my parents' house and said, 'You'll almost be as you were before.' He placed one arm on the kitchen counter, letting the other one dangle down like a pendulum, and began to rotate his shoulder, one way then the other. 'Do this every time the news comes on,' he said. Through the cloud of tramadol, I could only really focus on his swinging tie with its geometric patterns. My knee, he explained, would need to be put inside a 'machine a bit like a microwave', and my foot might always turn in a little from now on. I was a very compliant patient because I wanted him to like me, not because I was thinking of my body particularly. I was too high to think in terms of the future. When you're on tramadol, you forget there is a future.

One of the hardest things about the car accident was coming off the painkillers. No one explained to me what withdrawal was or that this could, in part, explain the ensuing depression. Or maybe it had been explained to me, but the information was too confusing through the chemical haze. Those pills were strong. For several months, I would try to stop taking them, only to panic and begin taking them again. It meant lying to the nice doctor with the patterned ties about how much pain I was in. Once he refused to give me repeat prescriptions, I had to make do with finding a chemist and buying anything that contained (your friend and mine) codeine. I thought I would be on them forever, incapable of imagining a solution. I texted a friend and said, 'Would it really be that bad if I just took them forever?'

On one of my first trips back to London, visiting a dear friend, after the realisation that I had forgotten to pack any codeine, I set off for the nearest Boots. I had to walk slowly because my head was throbbing and my legs ached. Suddenly I was sitting down on the pavement, my feet near the busy road, incapable of moving. A woman walking her dog asked if I was OK, her smiling face appearing over mine. 'Yeah,' I said, a bit embarrassed, 'I'm trying to come off these drugs is all.'

'That's the spirit,' she said, and walked on.

I'm sorry I lied to you and Anthony Canada, Becki. I didn't ever meet him, properly, but I did see him once, after one of our sessions, I think. He was on his knees, in a yellow vest, helping a woman in her forties to do a sit-up (a staple of the Anthony Canada Method), except he was actually looking at his reflection in the mirror. When she lifted her upper body, her stomach squished into folds. He eyed her stomach with a look of slight repulsion, before glancing over at the clock. She stopped, shook her head and said something like, 'I can't.' He said something like, 'We wanna get you a nice sexy flat stomach, remember?'

This vignette made me think about the time our usual netball lesson was cancelled, due to bad weather. Instead, exercise mats were put out in the school dining hall, and we were told to run around, and every time we got to a mat, to do ten press-ups. We'd had a supply teacher that day: a man in his forties possibly, but it was hard to say, due to my youth. All three of his forehead lines were quite deep, I remember. He stood in the middle of the hall, explaining to a room of fourteen-year-old girls that 'men like hard, muscular arms on a female. A nice toned arm is very, very desirable.' Notice the use of the word men here, not boys. One girl slipped on a pea on the floor that was left over from dinnertime, just an hour earlier, but still had to join in.

Maybe that's what put me off physical exercise. If it was simply a means to getting a boyfriend, then there were quicker ways. I lay on the disgusting mat, looking up at the teacher striding around watching us, and thought, 'He's probably turned on right now, the fucking perv.' I did one press-up and thought about how unfair the power dynamic in the room was, and that even if he was walking around turned on, there would be no way to know, and how, apart from an erection and dilated pupils, there was no other way to 'prove' that he was aroused, and how frustrating that fact was. Besides, what he said wasn't even true about toned arms. The most fancied girls in the year were: Louise, because she had developed breasts early and was the emotionally unavailable type (is there such a thing as an emotionally available fourteen-year-old?); Sarah, because she was physically available; Angharad, because she was rebellious and didn't give a shit; and Claire, because she was good at the Game Boy and had silky hair and a long neck. Arms were hidden under our school uniform at all times. Arms never came into it. The man was a fucking idiot.

As Anthony headed over to the water cooler in the corner of the gym, he had to walk past me, as I was tying up my shoelaces, and we briefly made eye contact. Even his eyelids looked muscly, like he smashes protein into them. But I also see a similar pain to mine. I knew that, under the right circumstances, it would be easy for Ant to fall in love with anyone. I made a note to myself to write a play about a personal trainer who falls in love with his client. The irony is, he falls for the very body he is trying so hard to change. If Anthony Canada could fall in love with a fat person, then maybe his whole universe would change. It would mean walking arm in arm down the road with a body that wasn't ideal, but he would have to tell the world that this was the body he had fallen in love with, and that maybe what he thought he needed and what he thought love would look like had been wrong all along. At the end of the play, the character of the personal trainer, 'Anthony', would make a moving speech about finally realising that he won't die from too much vulnerability after all, and that his large muscles were simply saying, 'Do you love me?' and that he was pumping up a chest that was lonely.

Anthony and I were the same. We were both desperately trying not to feel like victims. I was hiding away, he was puffing himself up. Both trying not to feel our own pain.

The woman in her forties lay back, breathing hard, awaiting further instructions. Ant gulped water from the fountain, and I saw a tattoo on his arm that looked like a medieval weapon. I wish him luck.

Becki, I really enjoyed feeling stronger and fitter, but that's only one type of strength and the sort I need isn't in a gym. It's like the way some writers think 'strong female lead' means a female character who is capable of violence/revenge, but it takes just as much strength to be fat or depressed. I appreciate the sort of strength you and Ant have – power that is amassed via physical discipline – but there's no point me feeling physically strong if I'm still trying to give away my power. It's like reading a book before you are ready. I need a bigger life first. I'm sorry I lied to you, Becki. It's a shame about the money, but I understand. I can't pretend that I'm taking ownership of my body by just going on a treadmill, it needs to start with the interior. Maybe we can try again in a few years, when I'm being a little nicer to myself? What's the point of all this fitness if I can't even take myself out for lunch?

Hope all well with you.

Katy

15

BROWNIES, OR, OXYGEN MASK

I used to like flying, but now the car accident had left me with an array of new phobias, including aerophobia, naviphobia (boats) and tachophobia (fear of speed). There is now a general sense of watching out for things that might go wrong. Sat next to me on the flight was a good friend. For some reason, I had never been able to be very truthful with this friend, about anything, but despite that I remained very loyal to her and to the friendship. Even with her being sympathetic, caring, smart, strong, witty and fun, she was still hard to talk to. Things were even a little formal between us. In the past, she had accused me of keeping secrets from her, but when I did try to reveal more of myself, she got scared and changed the subject. At around 35,000 feet I decided I wanted to try again, just after the teas and coffees and brownies were doing the rounds.

At the heart of it, I'm ashamed to say, was the fact that her mother had died when she was eleven, and I always felt as though I didn't want to burden her with my problems, because of this.

It's embarrassing to talk about mental health anyway: partly for the reason that I never thought I was allowed to, or that I had a voice, or that that voice mattered, and partly because of the term itself. Mental health used to mean something else to me. Until recently, I thought that the term 'mental health problem' could only be applied to very 'serious' and 'diagnosable' things like schizophrenia or borderline personality disorder. I had no idea that all the things I've struggled with in my life, namely depression, anxiety and addictive behaviours, would qualify to be called mental health problems. I'm elated that I get to say 'my mental health' now. It feels so good to say it out loud. It feels like a relief. A certain level of suffering had become so normal to me, it's only now I see that other people would have sought help, long before I did, unwilling to endure the anguish any longer than they had to.

Most people I know are struggling to take their own pain seriously.

I've always loved aeroplane food, but then I do tend to love most things that have been compartmentalised in a pleasing way. I don't know if it was the half a Valium talking, but about an hour into the flight I said to my friend something like, 'Things are . . . things are really bad at the moment.'

'What do you mean? They're really good though,' she said, tossing her hair back and looking worried.

'No, yeah, I know . . . they are, I suppose that's the thing. I don't feel like they are?' I said, smiling weakly.

'Well, they are,' she said, holding her stirrer in mid-air.

'Yeah, they are. But it's more that I can't access that feeling, the good feelings. It's like everything is covered in dark-grey icing.'

'Right. Actually, what do you mean?' she said.

'Well, I suppose I mean –' trying out the new phrase for the first time, with her – 'my mental health isn't very good.'

'I know people with mental health problems: believe me, you're fine,' she said, with a sort of full stop.

In moments like that, I would feel such rage against her, but I would, of course, hide it. It would suddenly dawn on me that she was selfish and didn't care about me and I would vow never to see her again, but then I always would. She must have had a hold over me.

But I also agreed with her. I thought that if I was 'functioning' and I wasn't trying to kill myself, then it wasn't serious enough to dwell on, and I was skilled at masking it by now. This is the dilemma of the high-functioning depressive. Maybe this hadn't been the time to tell her, flying through the air, at speed.

What struck me today, as a plane went overhead, is how similar her voice is to the internalised voice of my inner critic. I start to wonder if she has also been depressed all these years, and felt that she couldn't tell me. Perhaps we have both been leading double lives. She has always struggled to ask for help, so she might be resentful towards those who can.

It's always best when meeting new people to assume that they have a front-of-house life and a backstage life.

16

BIRTHDAY CAKE,
OR,
THE MOST POWERFUL FORCE IN THE UNIVERSE

We were already on the rum and Cokes, and it was only four in the afternoon. Most people were at work at this time. We had spent all morning painting one wall of his bedsit purple, and dancing around to Liberty X. Now we were slumped on his sofa, stoned, watching old episodes of Disney's *Adventures of the Gummi Bears*. He hadn't asked the landlord if he could paint the wall, but I think he sometimes enjoyed pissing people off, and I enjoyed being part of it. The sofa had a brothy smell, and little pouches of tobacco were piled up on one of the armrests. We were laughing at everything about the episode, apart from the bits that were supposed to be funny, because we weren't children any more. Our bracelets were matching: small red beads with a charm that dangled down, which we got from the hippy shop in the arcade a few days before. The rum was a joke really. It was too strong. We would sip it and then breathe in sharply as it stung the roof of our mouths. It was the only booze he could find in the small kitchen. The vodka was all gone. Vodka was his morning drink, diluted with orange juice, perhaps to give it that breakfasty feel. When we were teenagers, we spent as much time together sober as we did whilst pissed. But this was a few years on, and now he was drunk all the time, or never totally sober, one of the two. I would have imaginary conversations with him, in my head, just before I went to sleep, when I would either ask him why he drank so much or beg him to stop.

He told me that his nan had made him a birthday cake in the shape of a Gummi Bear, when he was little. I told him about the time my nan brought me back a bowl from Mykonos which turned out to be an ashtray. I was only ten. We laughed so much on his sofa.

In this episode of the Gummi Bears, they are stuck on an island, and they can't get home. They meet a sculptor Gummi Bear called Augusto. Instead of using the island's bamboo supply to build a bridge to get home, Augusto decides he needs it all to make a sculpture of a dragon. Even though Augusto is desperate to get off the island, he's stubborn and won't listen to the other bears. The Gummi Bears wonder why, if he's so homesick, he doesn't let them use the bamboo to make a bridge. He wants to get home, but he can't, the others conclude. And this was how I came to think about his drinking.

It's difficult when you are young and you come face-to-face with addiction. I knew nothing about alcoholism back then and didn't understand what it was. At first, I didn't even see it, or hear it, when he spoke. I didn't detect it, it was a slow build, like one long note, getting louder and louder. I noticed the silvery threads on his forearms from years of self-harm. A counsellor had told him to hold ice cubes in his hand, whenever he had the urge to cut himself. It short-circuits the brain, or shocks you out of your own impulses, or something like that, but I remember it helping only for a while. I knew he was in emotional pain. It was scary.

It was embarrassing to mention his drinking. I saw it as a phase. Best to let it play out, whatever he needs to do, before he's my old friend again. Then, as the drinking got worse, I was waiting and waiting for the plot twist, where he suddenly reveals that he had a plan all along, that the drinking was a way into something else, and a new, reformed person would emerge on the other side of all the destruction. But it was just more of the same. I felt powerless, which of course I was. I had no idea he couldn't stop.

I still haven't been to his grave.

17

CHIMNEY CAKE,
OR,
THE THOUGHTS I HAVE ABOUT CANCER WHEN
I OPEN MY FRIDGE DOOR AT NIGHT FOR A SNACK

1. I think this illness is a metaphor.

2. I think this illness is just a terrible illness.

3. I think it's both.

4. I think I knocked something off the table at 3 a.m., as I stumbled towards the fridge. I couldn't see that anything was broken the next day. Maybe a squad of mice carried away whatever it was.

The first time I went to the cancer ward, I had the kind of immature thought that some people didn't look like they had cancer. They looked quite well, nothing visibly broken.

5. I think there is no pleasure ... oh, look, a sell-by date that is also my birthday! It's a sign.

6. I think there is no pleasure to be had in remembering, as I always do at 3 a.m. as I stare deep into my fridge. I don't hate remembering, it's just something that happens when it wants, like abdominal bloating or loud music from passing cars.

When I was younger, I kept a diary because everyone else did, but it soon became stifling, like fitted waistbands.

7. I think it was good that I was told I had cancer first. It was my first ever paid acting job, in a way. I wasn't given many details about my character, just told which chair to sit on when I entered the room. The woman running the training programme said that when the medical student came in and delivered the news, I was to 'react realistically', so they could practise their communication skills. Medical role-playing was the official name for it. 'I'll be in the corner taking notes,' she said, 'but don't look at me, so that it feels as real as possible.'

The first med student rushed through it, as if he were late for something else. 'We found cancer cells in your womb,' he said. I put my hand up to my mouth. 'Am I going to die?' I asked. He quickly glanced at the course leader in the corner. She smiled with her mouth shut and gestured back towards me with her biro. I tried to make my hands tremble, to show them I was focused and in character. I asked if I could have some water, which I thought was a hyper-realistic reaction and probably what anyone would say if they had just been given this shocking news. He darted a side glance at the woman again, who subtly shook her head and gestured around the room with her folded specs, to indicate that it was a waterless room. As he explained my treatment plan to me, my stomach rumbled loudly, which seemed to impress everyone, like it had provided even more realism. The course leader looked pleased with how it all went.

The next student was a young woman who had gold

highlights in the front of her hair and the air of someone who did stand-up comedy, part-time. She moved the plastic chair so that she could sit closer to me – cross the divide. The course leader made a quick note of this. The trainee put her head quite close to mine. There was a smell, a sour apple scent, which I think was her body spray or deodorant. We locked eyes a little too intensely. This time it was throat cancer. I put my head in my hands and said that I was a teacher – I don't know why.

But when it really happens, it's nothing like this at all.

A few of us 'actors' went to the pub afterwards with the guy who I thought was in a rush to be somewhere else – the somewhere else turned out to be the pub. For the first half an hour, all the performers talked about the emotional impact of the simulations. We were a mixture of undergrads, retirees, wannabe actors and stay-at-home mums. Most of us smoked, including the med student. This was just before the smoking ban happened. In a pause, one of the mums said to the medical student, 'Whenever I see a medical person smoking, I think, "Ooh, maybe they know something we don't," like a secret trick for smoking without getting any bad side effects, and that's why they smoke too.'

'No,' the med student chuckled, 'I've got exams coming up, it's stressful, you know?'

8. I think I told someone once, 'If you feel like screaming, just have a yoghurt,' and they said, 'I'd like that on a fridge magnet.'

9. I think about that huge tree that fell down and landed a few inches from my front door last year, whilst I was sat,

miles away, in a noodle bar. My neighbour sent me a photo of the fallen trunk with the message, 'I thought a huge flood was coming or something, but I think it must have been the sound the leaves made as they fell – it sounded exactly like rushing water.'

10. I think it was eight or nine days after my father died that my mother heard a 'gunshot', on the stairs. When she rang to tell me, I said, 'It's probably something as simple as a drunk farmer in a nearby field scaring off a fox.' A few nights later, she called again to say that she could hear 'a choir'.

'Do you have a radio on somewhere?'

'No,' she answered, sounding scared, 'there's no one else in the house. There's no radio on.'

'Well, what were the choir singing?' I asked.

'Nothing,' she said, 'they were just warming up their voices, scales and things.'

A few days later, she collapsed on the landing, as she was carrying the ironing up. The noises were coming from inside her head. That's how I knew something was wrong. It had been a warning shot.

'Have you tried wailing?' the GP said, in her office, a few days later. 'Grief does strange things to folk, you know. People are scared to let it all out . . . like they do abroad.'

'I'm very familiar with the concept of somatisation,' I interrupted, 'I've been doing it for years. My body is the biggest barometer there is, but I don't think it's that.'

'Should I have a brain scan?' my mother enquired politely.

'I'm pretty sure it's just stress,' the GP concluded. There

was an empty chair in the corner of the room, with an oboe case leant up against one of its legs. The woman running the medical role-play training programme would have approved of a personal touch like that.

The only time I ever put an oboe in my mouth, a small piece of reed became imbedded in my lip and stayed there for four days. I was seven and it was my first anxiety attack.

11. I think the fridge light is the heart of any home: like the hearth that families would have gathered around long ago.

It's hard to imagine cakes of the future.

12. I think we weren't prepared for any more bad news. We sat on blue chairs in the hospital corridor, Mum and I, waiting to be given the results of the brain scan. I stood up. 'Don't leave me alone,' she said. I sat back down. She took some earrings out of her handbag and put them on, determined to get better. I reassured her and told her that all would be well, but my voice broke as I said it. In truth, I didn't know if auditory hallucinations were something dangerous, amazing or frightening. I didn't know what it all meant. I was hoping for a straightforward diagnosis of 'Joan of Arc' syndrome or something equally treatable and negotiable, but that's not what happened.

When the doctor delivered the news, he didn't move his chair around, he stayed on his side of the desk. *Growing* and *inoperable* were the words he used to describe her brain tumour, and all we could do was listen to the information he was reading from his computer screen. No one 'reacted realistically'.

'How long do I have left?' she gasped.

'It all depends on the rate at which it grows and if you respond to treatment,' he said, putting the cap back on his pen.

Once we entered the world of cancer, we also entered the world of cures. They were two separate ideas but with much overlap.

13. I think it's possible to overdose on cake, in one sitting. I read in the paper about a man in Swansea who died whilst taking part in a fairy-cake-eating competition.

When I open the fridge door at night, the first thing I feel is relief.

14. I think meeting cancer for the first time was a bit like meeting a famous dead person from history that I'd heard a lot about but never expected to meet. Perhaps not awe, but there was a sense that cancer was something eternal, that it would outlive us all; a power greater than everyone, even the doctors.

I suppose, deep down, I thought we had magical powers and that we were somehow immune from cancer. Which is another way of saying – I didn't think she could die.

15. I think about where all the ghostly night-time kitchen noises come from. The fridge is old and squeaking. Or maybe the mouse is back. It loves to sneak under the fridge, I've noticed.

16. I think it was a great comfort once we knew that we were powerless. I didn't read all the leaflets I was supposed to. There were so many. And forms to fill out and people to tell or 'inform' (to use the language of the leaflets). I dropped everything and moved back in to help care for her.

'In essence,' the oncologist began, 'we zap it or we cut it away. Those are always your two choices with cancer.'

On *This Morning* there is a feature about Kate Winslet paying for a woman's brain tumour treatment at an exclusive German hospital, offering something called immunology. It was going to cost £150,000. When the interview is over, I think, 'Well, I could sell my home, I suppose.' Later, when I mention the story about Kate Winslet to the oncologist, he says, 'Oh, it's too late for that type of treatment. It would be a waste of money.' In part, I was relieved that, when it was all over, I would still have a place to live in which to do my grieving, even if I won't have a mother (whose body was the first place I had lived). When I tell Mum about this interview, she is confused and thinks that Kate Winslet is trying to purchase the woman's tumour. 'She's changed,' my mother concludes.

17. I think worrying will soothe me, but it never does. There weren't enough hours in the day to do all the worrying I needed to do. I would wake up worried, then stay worried throughout the day and I'd still have worrying undone at the end of the day. In order to appear less crazed and self-absorbed, I even pretended to worry about the things other people were worrying about: climate change, the rise of global fascism, etc. But in truth there wasn't any room left in my body to take on the world's worries.

I bumped into an old friend on the Piccadilly Line. She was on her way to Mexico to buy 'rare herbs with healing powers' to cure her father, who was dying of stomach cancer. 'I started reading about these herbs in a thread on Mumsnet,' she began. 'There's so much evidence out there. It's the best chance we have.'

'Have for what?' I said.

'A cure,' she said.

She's in the world of cures, I thought to myself.

18. I think I was twelve when I first read about a famous dead nun called Julian. People quote her all the time without realising. She was extremely ahead of her time. She wrote things like:

All shall be well, and all shall be well, and all manner of things shall be well.

19. I think I need to go food shopping. I thought I already did. I wonder how long that jar has been in the fridge. The bottom shelf smells bad, like wet dog. There's a half-eaten tin of something, which is an easy way to get botulism, Mum always told me.

One oppressively hot night, Mum placed my pillowcase inside the fridge, a few hours before bed, to help me sleep. It was a 'clever trick'.

20. I think it all happened too quickly. It must have been in the early stages of the metamorphosis from my mother to cancer patient that I began working on this book. I sat and typed against a backdrop of steady beeps and hums from the machines around her bed. Her face was bloated now, her head bald. She went from Jane Fonda to Winston Churchill almost overnight. She wanted to look in a mirror. I googled 'where to buy chic headscarves'.

When writing, it's better to look away from an idea, because under direct eye contact ideas disappear. So I could only look at her from the side. I preferred to watch her watch the iPad, and pretend I was engaged with something too, but really I was just watching her. Everything was fine until we made eye contact, then it was all true.

21. I think I'm embarrassed about what I used to think of as stressful.

When the brain tumour was diagnosed, I thought, *The universe isn't done with us yet.* So this is what life is really like: a series of terrible events? I can't believe I was so in the dark for so long. The body is capable of betrayal at any given moment. But then I would ask myself: *Did someone promise me that it was going to be all good?* And the answer would be, *No, no one did.* So, then, where did I get this silly notion from that life was supposed to be all good and well? From a nun.

22. I think this is a terrible thing to think, but one Thursday afternoon some difficult thoughts came: *Did she cause her own cancer by drinking too much white wine, smoking too many cigars in the 1970s, not managing her stress and loving too much, to the point of extreme self-sacrifice?* She was so capable and knowledgeable. She hadn't caused her cancer, but she must have the answers, because she always did. She was doing really well until she lost the love of her life.

23. I think the reason I didn't go to Mexico to buy magic herbs was partly because my passport was out of date and it would've taken three weeks to get a new one. She might have been dead by then. Seemed counterintuitive. We didn't even

ask for a second opinion. Is that unusual? I think it's some-thing to do with growing up with (a) not a lot of money and (b) zero sense of entitlement. A friend of mine once told me that the reason she wasn't scared of flying was because of her overwhelming trust in and love of authority. I wasn't certain if we were being passive or realistic in our approach to the cancer. Cancer causes panic and desperation. People sent me links to articles about turmeric and CBD oil, which was very thoughtful of them, but there came a point where stories were no longer useful to us, just the truth of the situation. The pressure of time made every conversation we had vital. The chemotherapy was killing her brain cells, changing her, making her sleepy, forgetful and tearful. When the poison is administered, the patient knows it's working when they feel like crap.

24. I think it was after the second scan, we sat in the waiting room again, awaiting further results. Despite the air of quiet panic in the room, there is almost something com-forting about how easily I could recognise another cancer sufferer, particularly with tumour patients. A bloated face, from the steroids, and a totally or partially shaved head gave it away. Most sit in pairs, patient and carer. It's reminiscent of a vet's waiting room, with each anxious owner patting their beloved pet. Illness is infantilising, especially if you are old.

The best part of the waiting room was the volunteer worker who came round offering tea and cake, for free. She wore an apron, and her trolley was laden and heavy, so that when she pushed it she looked like she was trying to move it up a hill. Whenever she appeared, I had the feeling of normalcy and relief, as if I had been finally allowed back into my house, after being locked out. Everyone looked forward to seeing the trolley woman because she revitalised our souls. As we ate the rubbery cakes and sipped the warm tea, for a few moments we might forget where we were and why. At first, I thought that the free tea and cake was just for the patients, that my suffering would have been deemed insufficient to warrant a free tea and cake, but this wasn't the case, which was nice. It's important to acknowledge that carers suffer alongside the patient in separate but equally challenging ways.

I spotted a mother and daughter with exactly the same-shaped nose, tucking into a cupcake.

25. I think I was the sort of person who always loved going to other people's houses, looking for family in all the wrong places.

26. I think the more you know the less you know how to say it to people who don't know. Sometimes we had to unpack the language, as if the experts didn't want to frighten us. The way one doctor spoke, it reminded me of legal language. The higher up the doctors were, the less good they were at speaking in common language.

27. I think I heard this in a podcast: a depressed person tends to start a sentence with 'I', and once they begin to feel better, they will begin to use 'we' again.

28. I think I didn't care what the Airbnb looked like, I just chose the one closest to the hospital Mum was in. Because I can't drive, and because the taxis were infrequent and

unreliable, every morning I would do the long walk to the hospital with my backpack full of M&S sandwiches and small tubs of hummus. The backpack became a perfect symbol of the loneliness of being a carer and the ever-present physical and emotional weight of it all.

Becoming a carer is something that can happen very suddenly, without warning. 'A full-time job that you haven't applied for' is how I often heard it described by others. I was expected to learn a new medical language and new moves for safely lifting her out of the wheelchair. I had a sort of uniform. I wore virtually the same clothes every day, because I was too stressed to make decisions. Being a carer weakens you, like giggling does, except it's horrible. I walked up and down the same hospital corridors every day, with all the instincts of a careful sleepwalker.

29. I think women have always cared for the dead.

30. I think I overheard one woman ask if ringing the bell was compulsory.

Mum was lying down on top of the covers in the corner of the cancer ward. That's when I first heard the bell. The bell was rung every time someone was given the all-clear, and was cancer free. Over the next few weeks, it became just another detail, like the paper cups containing tablets, the water jugs, the light-blue gowns and the rush of activity when an alarm sounded. The bell attracted people. At first, when the bell sounded, patients would look up, straining their necks, wanting to see, then after a while people stopped looking. The staff cheered though. One day my mother said, 'There's a lot of resentment towards that bell in here.'

31. I think my friend finally believes that her cancer has gone. Even though she is still young and has been cancer free for six years, she said to me recently, 'No matter how hard I try I can't shake the feeling that I'm still ill. Every small ache I imagine to be cancer.'

My mother was the opposite: she never imagined it. I don't know what's worse: to imagine getting cancer every day and then one time it is true, or to believe that you are somehow exempt and then it happens to you.

32. I think about the woman in the bed next to Mum's. I learnt her name because the nurses repeatedly asked for her name and date of birth before they administered anything. Her name was Linda. Each time I passed by her bed, she would ask me for fags. I knew that I had some in the bottom of my backpack, left over from a party. I wrestled with the ethics of giving a cigarette to a cancer patient, but then I knew that she only had a few weeks left to live. When she was asleep, I placed a packet of Silk Cut Silver, containing two cigarettes, on her bedside cabinet. I could see a small knitted pouch just under her pillow. I didn't know what was inside, but thought it might be worry dolls. And I had the thought that replacing all one's cigarettes with worry dolls might be an effective way to give up smoking.

When Linda cried in the night, my mother would call out to her, 'It's all right, it's all right, Linda. Don't be scared.' Linda's son regularly visited and always brought spare fruit with him to give to Mum.

Linda died two weeks after the night I gave her my cigarettes.

Linda's son continued to visit Mum.

33. I think watching someone you love being watched is like watching yourself being looked at. When the doctor was listening to my mother, I would watch him, not my mother. I could never tell if she really knew she was going to die.

34. I think the fridge shelves aren't in the right place and I don't care. There was a segment on *This Morning* in which a tidying expert showed you how to organise your fridge properly. The presenter looked down at their iPad and, with big eyes, said to camera, 'Well, your fridge pictures are coming in fast from all around the country!' It struck me as a weird image and, perhaps coupled with the presenter's glee, I had a vision of people lining up their cameras with their fridges, like parents photographing their children on the first day of school. The expert said that she liked to store food in glass containers because then she could 'see what's in them'. A woman called in to say, 'My favourite part of my fridge is the cheese drawer.' I stare into my fridge, trying to find a favourite part. The expert then held up her label maker. I texted a friend and wrote: 'If I ever say I'm going to buy a label maker, please have me put down.' The expert demonstrated how to use the maker by sticking a label on to the middle shelf of the fridge that read, 'Eat me first'. I enjoyed the erotic undertone of the instruction, which seemed to be lost on everyone on screen.

35. I think my spirit animal is a monk that's been ill for six months. I was allergic to something in the Airbnb, the one near the hospital. I don't say anything but I clean the whole place, thinking it might help. It doesn't. I make

myself some soup and sit on one of the two hard wooden chairs. I can't find the TV remote, so I listen to the radio and look out of the window. Someone I slept with once was a guest on Radio 4. They are using a special, sensitive voice. They never used that voice with me. My mood nosedives dramatically. The world is against me, then. It's so boring being resentful. These days even when I see a 'closed' sign, I take it personally.

36. I think I'm obsessed with people's wounds.

I'm not at all sorry that we had so many parties in that house, but I do feel a pang of guilt when I think about the couple next door, Pat and Robbie. Pat told me over the fence one day that Robbie had testicular cancer and that he didn't need any more stress. We sent them a card and carried on with our young lives. The parties continued but were now a lot more sedate and infrequent. I was always fully anxious at the parties and would be the one to turn down the music every few minutes. Robbie began playing his pipe early in the mornings, in his back garden. He would start at about 6 a.m., sat on the patio, wearing a bandana that had flames up the side. I could see him out of the bathroom window when I brushed my teeth. I think he wanted to wake us up and let us know he was in pain, but it was fairly passive-aggressive. Fortunately the cancer was not aggressive and he was absolutely fine. He needed his pain to be witnessed, or at least heard.

37. I think I hurt her and myself. At first we tried to care for her at home. We tried for so long, but by this point she was virtually paralysed, because of where the tumour was

situated in her brain – the part that controlled movement. She could only really move one arm. This was the first time she asked me to find her a one-handed sewing machine. One day I dropped her as I was trying to transport her heavy body from the bed to the wheelchair. I hurt her and myself. We sat on the floor trying to catch our breath. I stroked her arm like she was a child. Her body had spoken: we could no longer look after it, we needed help. We packed up all her things and moved her into a hospice. When I was alone, I cried into a wardrobe so that I wouldn't add to her upset. As the tumour was getting bigger and stronger, she was disappearing.

38. I think about the graveyard I grew up next to. I would only go there during the day. It was large and difficult to navigate, because the paths were muddled like a brain.

39. I think her room was small and basic but I liked that it felt more like a Welsh cottage than a care home. It was homely with brown everything – carpets, textured wallpaper and armchair – but a colourful rug on the bed. In the middle of nowhere, I was reliant on taxis that stank of stale fags to get me there and back, but at least they were familiar with the twisty roads. 'You about to start your shift, luv?' they would ask as we approached the residential home, and then, upon explanation, 'Aw, I'm sorry to hear that, luv, you take care.'

She was sat upright in bed when I arrived, her eyes more red than usual.

The main side effect of all the chemotherapy and radio-therapy she had undergone seemed to be endless weeping, which in turn made me cry. The staff adored her and overflowed with love. They brought her ice creams and kissed her bald head with great affection and she was a hit in the day room. But the near constant flow of tears seemed too much even for them. Concerned members of staff would take me aside and comment on it, suggesting counselling or tougher meds. One of her friends came to visit and rolled her eyes when the tears started up again, for the fourth time, in one hour. I don't know, I felt it was appropriate. Why wouldn't you cry at the end of your life? Her rage, her discomfort, her distress – all these things were finally being expressed. She'll cry as many times as it takes.

Her nightie was just a baggy T-shirt. The dull white T-shirt was the only thing big enough I could find in her wardrobe to fit her expanding frame. I connected it in my mind with the white dress I had bought from a charity shop years ago, reduced to two pounds because of the subtle tea stain on the back. We both took real pleasure in making the dress as white as possible. We washed it again. It got whiter each time. And again.

40. I think my favourite mystic was allowed a cat, to keep the rats at bay. Julian was an anchoress. She was my favourite. She didn't just love God, she was in love with God. I think that's why I liked her, because she must have understood longing. Anchoresses were religious hermits. Some lived in tree trunks until they died, some in purpose-built 'cells' on the side of church buildings called anchorholds. One small window was allowed, through which they could glimpse the altar.

41. I think about when the poet Anne Boyer wrote: *I'd been*

making plans for a place for public weeping, hoping to install
in major cities a temple where anyone who needed it could get
together to cry in good company and with the proper equipment,
and what 'equipment' I would need.

I was a stoic kid. I liked *Newsround*, for example. I had
been trained from a young age not to show too much emotion in case it made those around me feel uncomfortable.
When other people fail to hide their emotions as well as I
do, I feel personally affronted. I become threatened by their
weakness and a little jealous of their bravery in showing it.
I try to eat cake a lot now as a political act, as a rebellion
against what I was taught, and, every time I do, I imagine this
is how others feel when they watch me eat cake. My English
grandfather had a cruel streak. I turned up to his funeral
wearing bright pink, still high from the night before, because
I hated him and myself. I sat at the back and I tensed my
whole body, refusing to cry, the taste of cheap cocaine still in
the back of my throat. The coke had been free, all I'd had to
do to get it was sit on some guy's lap, at a party. At the end
of the funeral, the vicar shook everyone's hand but mine.
He must have thought I was some slag who had wandered
in off the streets or something, but I was a blood relative.
How dare he. All I was doing was trying to express my hurt
and outrage through drug-taking and fashion choices, but
throughout the wake I was treated with derision and suspicion – like a childless millennial at Disneyland.

I didn't want my tears watched. I was never comfortable with that. I hated the thought of crying in front of
people. Then death changed everything. It rendered my

tears uncontrollable. What a burden sensitivity can be, but it's true that I never had the right equipment.

The equipment I would've liked for crying: soft tissues (not loo roll, which leaves a red mark if you drag it across an eyelid too roughly), painkillers for the immediate headache that comes from loss of water, water, a hairbrush, isotonics, a toilet nearby, pen and paper for the waves of thought, books, eyedrops, glasses (not contacts), a hand to squeeze, access to a secluded garden with birds and benches, a one-handed sewing machine and a contact lens case to catch my tears (we shouldn't waste water these days).

Towards the end, I would silently cry into a disgusting peach hand towel in staff toilets, because I wanted it to be over, and because I knew it soon would be.

42. I think about her friends coming to visit, with cakes in each hand. In the corridor outside her room, I prepare them: 'It's in her brain', 'it's terminal', 'she might cry', 'she might say something . . . not nice'. Then I leave them to greet one another, as I go off to find plates and a knife.

43. I think about why I don't remember something as important as its name. I forget the name of the particular type of tumour my mother had, but I do know that it was very right wing. I don't know if it's common to have a right-wing tumour, but hers was. As the cancer took command of her brain, she began to make increasingly bigoted comments, in a way that was not typical of my mother. So I think the tumour was to blame. This is because cancer cells are selfish. They don't do what they are told. I'm not claiming that all bigotry is due to brain damage, but in my

mother's case it was. When did I first notice the change?
Matalan probably.

On the side of the wheelchair-accessible taxi it said: 'We
take your stress away'. The driver dropped us right outside
the shop, but I couldn't really see because of the raindrops
still sitting on my glasses. We chose Matalan because it had
a ramp, but as I pushed Mum into the store, I suddenly
became aware of how vulnerable she was, now that we were
outside of the care home. It was just us now, no nursing staff
to help. The store and the other shoppers became a series
of spaces and objects to negotiate as we struggled our way
around the rails of clothes. People smiled and gave way to
us. They even looked a little concerned. We must've looked
like we didn't know what we were doing, and we didn't.

I began filling the trolley with large practical clothes,
anything that would accommodate her extra weight from
the steroids. We get excited about the bargains, hold things
up and comment on the feel of the material. For a brief
moment, we forget and it's like I'm a teenager again: when
supermarkets started selling clothes and I would hold dresses
up against me and ask, 'Do you think this would fit me?'
and she would say, 'Maybe.' Shopping for clothes has always
been about an imagined future.

The wheelchair keeps getting in the way of other customers. 'Long sleeves for when I have visitors,' Mum
instructs me. Her arms were almost totally the colour of red
wine because the skin was so thin now and bruised easily.
She pointed to the top shelf:

'And I need a figure-hugging hat too, like that one.'

'I'm not sure you can describe a hat as figure-hugging,' I said.

'Oh, you know what I mean, one that doesn't let in the draft. My head gets cold.'

Now I spend a lot of time staring at the top of her head.

She began commenting on people's appearance, as we turned a corner, but then the commentary progressed to something worse, more distasteful. It was the point at which the right-wing tumour had won. It was like the point of no return in a film. She was never quite the same after this.

Outside, it was still raining, we were slipping about on the narrow, Welsh pavements. I was shocked to discover how ill equipped the small market town was to deal with wheelchairs and all too aware of how privileged I was, that I'd never had to deal with this problem before. When I discovered that a lorry had parked right next to a lowered pavement (all of which we were completely reliant on), blocking our only route into M&S, I felt my nails dig into the palm of my hands. We were stranded on the pavement, our clothes soaked through, exhausted. When the lorry eventually moved, the driver didn't even notice us. We were minor characters in his day.

M&S was packed and we didn't have much time. Just inside the door, a well-dressed woman was collecting money for a cancer charity, stood next to a large cardboard banner with facts about cancer on it. I asked if I could leave Mum with her for five minutes, with the brakes on, whilst I quickly did some shopping. Mum wasn't really supposed to be alone in case she had a seizure, or worse, but I knew it would take too long to push the knackered wheelchair around the aisles with me. The well-dressed woman pulled an inconvenienced face. I wanted to say, 'But I thought you wanted to help cancer? This is cancer.'

At first, I had considered Mum's small beige room to be her prison cell, sealed off from life, but now that we were back in it, this was no longer the case. The new reality was that the room protected her from the outside. The staff welcomed us back with tea and cake, which arrived on a tray from the kitchen that smelt of tea and soup. She is home and I love the rain.

44. I think she never recovered. The night her parents sent her away to boarding school, she clutched her little doll close to her chest and cried herself to sleep. She was small, frightened and vulnerable. When her daughter was born, she became that doll for her. She will have a hard time putting it down from now on.

45. I think three, maybe four, different men turned up to tell her they had always loved her.

46. I think it was me who once said, 'Never learn people's first names, or they might fall in love with you'.

47. I think Pandora actually opened a 'jar', but it's often mistranslated as 'box'.

48. I think about how the drivers are.

I made the journey to the care home countless times and began to enjoy the wisdom of the taxi drivers, who notice me weaken as the months go by. They are typically older so more likely to have experienced great loss, and I look forward to their over-shares. 'I was in Debenhams when I found out my dad was dead,' one man tells me in a thick Valleys accent, 'but I didn't deal with the emotional side, you know, and a year later I had a stroke,' and, 'You're doing everything you can, love, trust me.'

At night the country lanes were dark, all you could see was the occasional pair of cow's eyes, lit up by the car's headlights.

49. I think it was me who once said, 'To grow up is to lose everything once.' I think I might have said it in a Ryman's, just quietly to myself, and simultaneously to the universe, which is all too easily done.

50. I think about why Mum and I spent seven years pretending I didn't smoke.

51. I think about what the fridges in happy homes look like.

52. I think the fridge is too cold.

53. I think of her brain like a network of connections, like the internet.

I think chemo must affect the part in charge of language. Her brain slowed, just like my father's did.

When I was growing up, whenever the internet was slow in our house she would say, 'That'll be America coming online,' no matter what time of day it was.

54. I think one of the staff tells me that it's important to maintain a life outside of cancer and do nice things, so I visit an art gallery near to where I live. In the gift shop they sell small vases. They range from three inches all the way up to five. When I asked the girl working there how much they were, she said, 'This is only my second day.' They were

displayed on a white shelf in order of size from smallest to largest, left to right. All of them blue. As I leave, a boy member of staff tries to engage the girl member of staff in conversation. 'Can you do impressions?' he asks. She makes the sound of a whale. It's convincing enough to shatter the vases. He thinks for a moment, then does an impression of Jay-Z's laugh. It's good to treat myself. Good to get out.

Because all my closest friends were busy, I was forced to meet with a less close one: still good, but not the ideal. This particular friend repeats the same anecdotes over and over again. I don't mean in the same sitting, but every time I see him, the same stories, every time, like a hurt lover doing an autopsy on a past relationship. In some of the stories, I was actually there; they are 50 per cent *my* stories, but he tells them as if I hadn't been there at all. Doesn't he see my confused expression? I don't know how much more I can take.

55. I think of these women who gave themselves to a life of seclusion and enclosure – the anchoresses. For them it was a living entombment, living in their cell until the physical body dies. And I thought of all the afternoons together, as if they were one: brushing her teeth, gently tilting her head towards the cup to spit in so it wouldn't spill on her fluffy leopard-print dressing gown and how this was the room she would die in. This isn't how I had imagined her death.

The same theme tune from the same quiz show came floating through the walls every day at 5 p.m. It was like the normal world was colliding with our new world. A lot of our conversation revolved around crumbs and where they were hiding. Her world had shrunk to just a few objects.

My job was to rearrange them several times until she was satisfied. By this time she could only move her left arm. I had bought several items, online, for one-handed people, like a knife and fork combination cutlery set and a device for pulling up socks, but a one-handed sewing machine was impossible to find. She became obsessed with the idea, even though we both knew that she wouldn't ever sew again. She would ask me to hold up a piece of paper whilst she drew out her design for a one-handed sewing machine. Then she made me promise to patent it and make a prototype, after her death.

'How much does it hurt on a scale of one to ten?' she was asked.

The language of pain isn't helpful. The placement of pain, on a scale from one to ten, relies on having been in pain before. When I imagine a psychopath, even a nice one, I see them always in the colour red, giving scores of ones and twos. Have I invented this fact or is it logical to assume that psychopaths don't feel their own pain?

56. I think when doctors described how cancer cells operate, it sounded like they were describing a mystical force. No one can say for certain why cancer cells behave the way they do.

One of the oncologists was very arrogant and we didn't like it when we had to speak to him, which was not very often. 'He acts like he's God's brother,' Mum said.

57. I think about if I'll be asked to go on *Celebrity Bake Off* once this book comes out, the stand-up-to-cancer one.

58. I think about the sounds: the birds outside, the game

show that played again and again, the low hum of the bed that sounds like a fridge-freezer, and the mechanical plates that move her legs for her every few minutes so she won't get bedsores, like she's at sea. The body is not designed to stay still for that long. But the light is beautiful. 'Open the window a little,' she says.

Turning her head towards me, she says, 'How will I know when it's happened?'

'I think you'll just know,' I say.

'I want to be someone, but I don't know who I can be any more,' she replies. 'How will I know when I've died?'

Where is this pink one-handed sewing machine?

59. I think about when the priest visited and it made her angry. Mum had never reversed her opinion that religion was a coping mechanism for the weak. Who needs religion when you have white wine, romance and your children. These things had been her salvation.

60. I think the fridge light might cure my seasonal affective disorder. I feel like a cow caught in the headlights, staring into it at 3 a.m.

61. I think about laughing sometimes.

She went on gripping, with her one good hand. I watched knackered strangers pull up her pants. The skill I have in all of this was witnessing. I didn't turn my head away much. I wanted to observe it and really see this death happening. There is no pink one-handed sewing machine.

62. I think about when an inspector visited the care home and was concerned by how much cake the residents were consuming. *Cake is not part of a healthy diet*, she had written

in her report, but she was missing the point. The home-made cakes were a sign that someone cared. It wasn't an act of neglect, it was one of love, of Welsh hospitality. Often the cakes went uneaten, but it was about normalcy, ritual.

I loved to see her eat cake with such passion, for the first time ever. I'm just sad that illness was the explanation.

But, overall, I think cake blunted our wish to talk about macabre things. Cake was a distraction as painting her nails was a distraction.

The last cake she ate was a mini-Battenberg, and the last book I read to her was by Audre Lorde. We only managed to get through half of *Sister Outsider*. 'No one can learn to write like that,' was her verdict, 'that's something you're born with.' I mention this because I have often wondered if the last book you read is important. I remember the last book I read to my dad too, but I'm too embarrassed to tell you. The last book you read before you die is like the type of coin that gets put under your tongue for Charon. It is mental substance for your journey, something to remember as you go on your way. When she meets the ferryman, in place of gold or silver she will be able to quote Audre Lorde, which I think will be more useful to her and will ensure safe passage.

63. I think about the little drawings I did of her, absent-mindedly, as she slept. Her black arms made it look as though she was decaying from the outside in. There was one window in the room, which afforded her views of birds and the tops of trees. She was so sad to be away from nature. I tried to take her back to the beach so many times, but it had been a disaster. I've always liked what Tracey Emin said

about the body wanting to be in nature: *I couldn't be in the landscape, but I could be with myself. I'm flesh, I'm blood, I'm water. I'm all these structures which are completely nature. I was the nature.*

It was her feet that made me want to weep the most. The point at which a person no longer requires shoes is a turning point. A sign that it's over.

64. I think I knew we were nearly at the end when her dog got a tumour as well. The dog starts to follow me around. We have previously had no relationship at all, but now it knows that something's up, and that I'm the person who will acknowledge it.

65. I think that every time I was going to the care home now, I was wondering if it was goodbye, and every time I said 'goodbye' if that would be the last time I said it. This makes me constantly tense. My friend A says that I can't think like this, it's too much pressure, and that, in time, the last moment won't be the only memory I focus on. This is good advice.

Death requires faith, I suppose, because even with the luxury of time to prepare, it still seems far-fetched and absurd.

All you can do is wash your face and get all the relevant documents in order.

66. I think about why it seems to be the women of my mother's generation who have said the most upsetting things to me over the years, and yet they are the generation the least likely to talk about how hard motherhood is.

67. I think that … well, I'm sorry to tell you, but the camera hates you.

68. I think about the time a little giggle came from behind the toilet door. I recognised the sound as Maude's voice. She haunted the corridors like a little shadow, every day. She was very pale and never went anywhere without her red handbag and gold watch. She would gently whimper and cry to herself as she slowly walked the halls. Occasionally, I would go and retrieve her, guiding her back to her room. If you touched her right arm, she would point at her watch with her left and say, 'It tells the time lovely,' using 'lovely' as an adverb.

When I got to the toilet door, I could see that it was slightly ajar. That's when the smell really hit. When I pushed it fully open, Maude was naked and had shat all over the floor, like a horse. She looked up at me and smiled. But what was more shocking to me was seeing elderly genitalia, up close. It seemed like a rare site and so taboo. It was educational. In my life, in terms of older women's bodies, the point where the circles meet in a Venn diagram would contain high art and leisure centres.

On my way out, I overhear a grandfather asking his grand-daughter to 'go a bit blonder' for him. 'You know I love it,' he says. It was harder to stomach than the smell of shit.

Getting to be old must be like heading out in a straight line from a city, deep into the countryside: you can hardly believe you're on the same piece of land, it looks and feels so different.

69. I think about the last few hours we sat with her, stroking her hair, adjusting the angle of her pillows. I was so full of love for her. The room was so full of love.

70. I think the house of death has but one door, but it's the windows I don't like.

71. I think about the fact that my fridge has a better energy rating than me.

72. I think I used to think that being thin was like having money, but now I think being smart is the new thin.

73. I think the moon is a cake, the sun a syrup.

74. I think about her slow, heavy breathing. A few days before the end, I had a sense of being trapped in the room with an entity, rather than my mother. She stared up at the ceiling and said:

'It's back.'

'What's back?' I asked.

'Some flesh, dangling by its legs,' she said quietly.

'Can you see anything else?'

'Yes.' she said. 'Black wings.'

It was so strange that I wrote the exchange down the moment she fell asleep. I wouldn't say it was supernatural, I would say it was the brain shutting down, but for a brief moment it was as if we were trapped in an anchorhold with some demons.

I start to see images of entombed women everywhere. There were more anchoresses than anchorites. Maybe women felt safer in cells than they would wandering around medieval Britain. Maybe they felt protected. Getting bricked up in a small room by a church is still preferable to dying in childbirth, being under male control or a long shift of egg collecting.

75. I think about my friends and how much I care about

them. And maybe I withhold expressions of appreciation sometimes, because it's embarrassing or because I assume it's a given. The one thing I don't have is a great friend who is an older woman, an artist perhaps, someone to be a mentor, who's had loads of therapy but is not overly sincere, politicised but also happy. She loves herself, but the friendship feels equal. Her house is clean and just the right size and we live just the right distance from each other so that the friendship is in no danger of becoming too intense.

76. I think about the friend who texted me to say that a sense of the absurd is essential if you are to cope. And we all know that some cope, and some don't. Death forever changes a person. Being alone is important. Ultimately, it is a quiet, internal process of coming to terms with change that no one else can do for you, and no one will be aware that the process is happening but you.

77. I think about how my muscles seemed weaker, despite always walking everywhere and tidying and doing. I was compulsively checking my phone. Normal TV was too intense for me, too contrived. No dramas, no scripted comedies either. I couldn't handle the sight of someone who had their shit together, someone who you would want to be, with professional make-up or lighting. It agitated me and seemed so mocking and false. I couldn't bear to look at anyone with a normative body. I was attracted to unstable bodies. I found myself watching documentaries on YouTube about weight-loss surgery patients, crying along with their tiny successes and failures.

Watching people coming round from anaesthetic was

strangely comforting. It seemed to capture the combination of intimacy and coldness of hospitals. I went in search of anything with real people. I flicked around the channels until I found things like *GPs: Behind Closed Doors*. The world of doctors and medical care had become so familiar that I didn't want to let it go, it provided me with a sense of continuity after Mum's death. I longed for transformation stories, ones where the story went from bad to good or, even better, from bad to good to bad to good again. I was less interested in from good to bad.

78. I think about all the objects in her room. Her shoes still contain the groove of her feet. Her handbag contains a mirror and some tissues. Who does this handbag belong to now? This handbag doesn't have an owner any more.

79. I think how, despite what the oncologist, nurses and relatives in the WhatsApp group said, I held on to the hope that she might recover. Even though I watched her die every day. I think I held on to this belief right up until the moment she died. I thought I was prepared for her death but it was still shocking. We looked so alike that it was a mirror to my own mortality.

80. I think about the empty wheelchair.

I was once filming a sitcom in front of an audience and no one was laughing. A boy in a wheelchair was sat right at the front with his dad. The boy sounded like he was upset. We kept having to do take after take because the boy's cries were interfering with the sound. When I asked the producer if we should do something, he said, 'That noise means he's enjoying it.' The script was so bad that I honestly don't think anyone was enjoying it. They moved the boy and his father to a 'nicer' area, but in reality it was just so he was further away from the microphones. I remember thinking that if I just told the *Guardian* about them being moved, the whole show would get cancelled and I could go home. The noises he made were the most humane aspect of the entire evening.

81. I think that when a character is supposed to be fun in a movie they close the fridge door with their hip. I can't do that with my fridge because it only comes up to the height of my vagina, which is a good six inches from my hip bone.

82. I think it's probably worse to be bored in your own language. If I'm going to have to watch a boring play, I'd rather it be in another language. We were in a beautiful old theatre in either Buda or Pest, I forget which, watching the opening night of a play by a well-known Hungarian playwright. I only knew the Hungarian for 'yes', 'no' and 'thank you'. I was seventeen, and had gone with my mother on a trip to visit one of her oldest friends, who had returned to Budapest after many years and now worked in theatre administration. The theatre was freezing, temperatures that Dorothy Perkins jackets were not made to withstand. The play was set in rural Hungary and seemed to involve politics, shouting and some plastic lambs. On either side of the stage, two naked actors, covered in white chalk, continuously ran on the spot. It was a three-hour play. They were running a marathon every night, like Eddie Izzard did for Comic Relief, but their cause wasn't charity, it was art. I tried to imagine what they did in the interval.

Afterwards, at the drinks reception, held in a heavily

curtained room, I asked the director of the play to explain the plot to me, but she simply said, 'There is no need to translate.' I asked if the giant rotating cog that descended at the beginning of act two represented 'the crushing wheel of capitalism'. 'No need to translate,' she said again. I thought perhaps it was a bit like converting to Judaism, and that I should ask a third time to show I was serious:

'Was the play about the life of Eddie Izzard?'

'There is no need to translate this play . . . it is pure experience.' It was a similar feeing to this when we had to deal with 'God's brother' at the hospital.

The two naked actors were now more clothed and sat drinking at the bar with their heads close together, giggling, like they could read each other's thoughts, which must be what happens once you've jiggled naked in front of someone for hours. All the actors were smoking and swearing and not smiling. I stared at them, studying the way they moved, working out how many calories a day I would need to consume to look like them.

A Dobos cake was carried in as part of the celebrations, and the director gave a short speech in Hungarian and held up a plastic glass of wine as a toast. The many-layered cake put me in mind of 'The Princess and the Pea', a story I always found plausible, or at least informative, as a means of sensitivity testing. The cake was impressive, but the actors' bodies were the main event, to me. They didn't really notice me slouching near to them, in my size sixteen jeans, with my schoolgirlish hair that wasn't quite long enough for a ponytail. One of them flung out her arms as she talked, for emphasis, and I deferred to her body by moving out of the way each time.

I thought to myself that I was born to be part of this. Here was the European avant-garde scene I had read about in books, full of artists and witty conversation and people who were smart and pretty in all languages. I finally knew what I wanted: a life of the mind, but to be touched up a bit as well.

The following afternoon, I walked around a Christmas market in the old town. Ancient-looking women sold hand-knitted gloves that spilt out of wicker baskets. A girl about my age, head to toe in denim, waved a Coke can dipped in glitter in front of my face, trying to sell it to me. I think it's a Christmas decoration and I politely decline. The place smelt of pine and cinnamon.

Mum and I had argued during our continental breakfast at the hotel, so we were giving each other space. Every once in a while, I would glance over to check on her, on the other side of the market. She was going to buy something called Chimney cake, on the recommendation of her friend in arts admin. Chimney cake was so called because of its cylindrical shape.

There was a group of young drunk guys in the middle of the square, shouting and laughing in a way that was just starting to annoy people. I walked across the square towards where Mum was. After a few steps I felt myself being pushed forward and my feet suddenly leaving the ground. One of the young men had run up behind me, put his head between my legs and was lifting me up on his shoulders, gripping my thighs tightly with his hands. It happened so quickly that there was no way of stopping him. I shrieked just before he had time to unfurl to his full height. He lowered me back down, and ran away laughing. I could still feel the pressure between my legs where his head had been. I quickly walked away in case they followed.

I couldn't see my mother. She had left the Chimney cake stall. I stood still, rehearsing in my mind how I would describe what just happened. Then I spotted her in the crowd, but something was wrong. An older woman was hassling her. Suddenly she punched Mum in the stomach and quickly grabbed her handbag. But then something extraordinary happened: my mother let out a cry – the likes of which I've never heard before – a terrible sound, her face distorted with anger, and the sound that came out of her mouth was like an animal in great pain. Her fists were clenched. The older woman looked so shocked and scared that she very calmly handed the handbag back to my mum.

The experience was so powerful that I felt like I was punched too.

Years later, I would make the same noise, when she died.

18

WELSH CAKES,
OR,
HAND-WRITTEN LETTER TO A BEST FRIEND THAT I'LL NEVER SEND

Dear Best Friend,

It's funny that when people ask us when we first met, we each begin to tell a different story. You say it was early-morning break and that I was standing in the triangular gap under the stairs with another girl, called Jo, and that as you walked past I looked at you and said, 'We're contacting the Devil, wanna watch?' Then Jo and I took each other's hands, closed our eyes and began slowly counting backwards from thirty. But the scene was interrupted by the maths teacher, the one with the bulging eyes, who said, 'What's going on here, then?' We quickly dropped our hands, and Jo looked down at her shoes and then said softly, 'We were contacting the Devil, sir.' The maths teacher paused, and then said, 'Well . . . don't.'

My version is that we met when the same teacher said to us, in a disgusted voice, 'You two stay behind.' He bollocked you first. The reason why you were in trouble was because you had shouted the word 'foreskin' during morning assembly. I was there because I had continually lied about using a ruler when drawing a diagram. Something about standing next to each other made us desperate to giggle. I swear we had never spoken before that.

We both agree, though, that the next time we saw each other was when we chatted on the edge of the out-of-bounds woods that surrounded our comprehensive, where people went to be kissed. On that day, though, we had gone there to smoke rollies and listen to an album.

I know we haven't spoken in a while, four years now, but I do think about you a lot. Sometimes I'll think about you for several days in a row.

Do you remember how, even though we would spend every lunchtime together, we would still rush home to speak on the phone after school and I would say, 'I can only be an hour,' but it would always spill over and our mums would say, 'What do you two find to talk about for so many hours?' We couldn't even answer, because it would all be wiped clean, and we'd start again the next night anyway. But not jokes, jokes could always be repeated. Our mums said that they always knew when we were on the phone to each other because of all the laughter coming out of our rooms. Back then, it was impossible to imagine a day going by without us speaking.

Before we move on, though, I want to tell you that I love you. I just didn't want to miss that out, because that is important to say.

The last time we spoke, I told you that I would go to the Post Office to demand an explanation as to why the birthday card you sent me never arrived. And I did go. They said that they were very sorry, nothing they could do, blah blah. I even tweeted them. And, of course, I believe you when you say that you definitely sent it. I would KILL to be able to read that card now. KILL. The reason I still fixate on that birthday card, I think, is because of what you said about the message within. You said it wasn't just jokes. You said it was actually 'deadly serious and I wrote about how you've stuck with me through everything and how I think you're amazing and stuff like that really'.

It might still show up, even though that was four years ago and I'm at a new address now. There was something else that you said that day too, but I'll come back to it, if that's OK.

I passed that pub the last time I was in Cardiff. The one we'd meet up in, when I'd come home from university. It's looking pretty sad. A few of the windows were smashed in, like the pub itself had been in a fight and lost a few teeth. It was always pretty rough though. We spent an afternoon there once, tucked away in a dark corner, on the seedy red chairs, trying to go unnoticed. We sat for hours, smoking and drinking and talking, whilst they played the Stereophonics album twice through. A man with a scar on his forehead joined us, uninvited. He told me that I looked like a singer, I always remember that bit, then he tried to get with me, then you, then both of us, then neither of us, then gave up. Later we saw him outside, holding a newspaper over a dog's head to protect it from the rain.

I didn't talk much about university life and you didn't talk about your unhappiness, or what you were doing or taking to deaden your pain. Escapism was our priority. I liked that about our friendship. Did you? Sadness disappeared quickly when we were together. But now I wonder if I asked you enough questions about your life or if you didn't want me to. I knew that you had started an art foundation course, but that you weren't enjoying it or you were falling behind, and you were spending more and more time hanging out in the park, next to the castle. Even though things went unsaid, we still managed to make each other feel loved. We tried to give to each other the love we couldn't always feel for ourselves.

Whenever I talk about you, and I love talking about you, the first thing I mention is what a talented artist you are and how vast your imagination is. You always had very bold ideas. I think you always knew that you were bright, and didn't need to prove it, but were frustrated that your mental health limited your options. I will never forget how frightened you were when the government, unfairly, claimed you were fit for work, when you clearly weren't.

Even though I talk about you a lot, it's weird how you change quite often in my memory.

After it happened, I did need medication for a while. I hadn't needed it for a few years. I'm not blaming you, I'm just letting you know. It was because I missed you so much, but your absence was for me to deal with, not you. When I went to pick up the antidepressants, the pharmacist recognised me from TV, and there was something very shameful about it. The more he complimented me, the more I had to say thanks, but sort of shrug and gesture at the tablets, as if to say, 'OK, well, obviously I don't agree, sir, or I wouldn't need these . . .'

When I got home, I put the tablets in the small medicine cupboard, then I pulled all the towels off the racks, threw them on the floor and screamed.

One of the things that I am most proud of about our friendship is how strong and deep our connection became, particularly as we went from our twenties into our thirties. A new level of disclosure, intimacy and trust had appeared. We continued to speak on the phone, nearly every day, even up till a few days before it happened. I loved hearing about all your future plans, like how you thought you might go back to college or look into becoming a Buddhist.

It was a bit stressful when you came to visit me in London, only because I knew how much you hated the Tube, and how strict your daily self-care routine had to be, so you didn't visit me much, and you only liked Camden anyway, when you did come. That one weekend at mine was the only time we got pissed off with each other, but we couldn't bear to fall out, so we forgave each other quickly.

The last time you came to visit me in London, as I waved you goodbye from my doorstep, I remember thinking that it was OK to stop worrying about you, because I knew that the final series of *Peep Show* would be out soon, and that was something you were really looking forward to.

During our last phone conversation, you said something a little mysterious. You said that you had something to tell me, something that I 'wouldn't believe'. 'You won't believe what's been happening,' you said, but you wanted to tell me, another day, but I said, 'No, tell me now,' but you were too tired, you said. That was on Tuesday and then you were dead on Thursday. What was it you were going to tell me?

I think because you died very suddenly, without warning, is why I have been angry. But whenever I saw bereavement counsellors, they looked so pleased with themselves when they got me to admit that I was angry with you and I would think to myself, 'They're not that smart,' but I would let them think that it was a breakthrough for both of us. I haven't stayed angry.

Jo drove me to your funeral. She is a really incredible friend. I think you would love how close we have become. I wish you could have seen your service and how many came. I think it would have overwhelmed you. You were the one person I would have liked to have shared that day with.

There were a lot of people there. The room was full. Jo and I had to sit at the back, because we had got a bit lost on the way and there were no seats left. I wore a dark-blue dress, and I know you wouldn't have cared that it wasn't black. My coat was black, though, and I kept that on. Most people kept their coats on, because it was October in South Wales. Jo and I held hands the entire time.

All the people that we secretly took the piss out of from school were there, and some of the lush people too that we liked, but you would have found it funny. A few of our mutual friends turned round and nodded at me, as if to say, 'I'm sorry,' and I nodded back. Everyone looked so old. I'm ashamed to admit this but when I saw how devastated some people were who weren't that close to you, I thought, *But you weren't even his best friend, I was, and if you can be and look that upset, then how must I be and look?* It scared me.

It's so weird that you died.

A nice man with a calm voice got up and began the service, but he was a stranger all the same, and it was an adjustment – the fact that he was talking about you, but had never met you. I don't know what you would have thought of that. I wanted him to shut up, because he didn't know you. It should've been me talking because I knew you the best. It was lonely to be there without you. If only love can be measured, then I could have got up and just said the number of the measurement of our love into the microphone, and then everyone would have understood why a number was all I could bring myself to say.

But I didn't get up and say a number, I didn't say anything. That's why I am writing this. I wanted to apologise for not speaking at your funeral, and I'll try to explain why I didn't.

I couldn't look at your coffin directly, not straight away. But I felt as though no one wanted to, but everyone knew it was there. Oh my God, D, that was you up there, in a box. Even when I looked directly at it, I was still secretly thinking, *But I'll call you tonight as normal, though, right?*

I don't think I had ever really appreciated the full ergonomic horror of coffins before. I wish it hadn't been so you-shaped, if you see what I mean. I wish it hadn't been so obvious that you were in there. There was nowhere else you could have been. And I thought about all your tattoos and piercings and what they must have looked like on a body without life. I would never see your skin again, the soles of your feet, your small ears. I tried to come to terms with every part of you that I wouldn't see again. The funeral made everything very real.

You and I once joked about which of us would die first. 'It's bound to be me,' you said, 'because, you know . . . I'm a bit . . .' But you never finished the sentence and then we just laughed at how strange and morbid we were being. I often think back to that conversation now.

I'm sorry that I didn't say anything at the service. I hadn't quite realised how reliant we were on each other. I had stupidly thought that, all these years, it was me who was supporting you. I was struggling to physically talk or stand on that day. I was so proud to be your friend and jealous of any new friends that you made, who got to discover you from scratch. I was sat at the back. I needed to mourn privately that day, and I hope you understand. I couldn't talk.

This is what I would have said. I would have talked about your acute sensitivity. I marvelled at your ability to empathise with and understand others. I would have talked about your strength and intelligence. How you were funnier than most professional comics that I know. How you were a good and loyal friend and how we understood each other. I would have talked about how you could be friendly and charming one moment, and then shy and furious the next. I would have mentioned your excellent memory and how you remembered my life too, so that I could ask you about things that had happened to me, when I couldn't remember them. I would have talked about going to my first concert with you and rolling down big hills in West Wales with you, creating a lot of mess with you and being late all the time and getting told off a lot with you and how much you had to change your life and you just got on with it and were brave about it. I hope I told you I loved you enough times. I'm sorry that I cancelled meeting up with you in June. I'm sorry that I didn't manage to get through to you that night. You didn't answer your phone to me, which was so unusual. You were a true friend. I wish we hadn't pretended that we were both fine, on the phone to each other, for so long. At the time of your death, I loved you more than ever. The measurement of love would have been at its highest.

At the reception bit afterwards, people wanted to talk to me and they were kind and sweet. We were all saying the same things really – words of love and shock and sadness and support. Everyone was acting quite rationally though. No one was screaming, for example. We all talked about you, D, and how we weren't going to see you again. When I saw the large pile of Welsh cakes, all kneeling on top of each other, on a big plate, I realised that there have been Welsh cakes at every funeral I've ever been to. In fact, it's the only time I ever eat them. And I watched your beautiful young child giggling, running around and biting into one of them.

I find myself absorbing your traits. I eat the foods you like and I use your favourite words. I say our jokes to myself. And I've come up with some new ones for us too.

I miss you in a way that feels like a very intense craving.

Grief is so strange, D. You get asked to do podcasts.

I love you, my dear friend.

19.

FRUIT CAKE,
OR,
A JOYLESS LIFE

After Mum died, one of her friends came round to see me with a fruit cake. As I put the kettle on, I wondered if she was nervous or not about us meeting. Our only link in life was this person who didn't exist any more. I put two slices out for us on my best plates and placed a small table closer to her knee, to place her tea on. I was happy to listen to her talk about her grief – she had travelled a long way to be here. I pretended to be interested in the details of her journey and nodded and agreed with things that I didn't think were true or I had heard before about loss. She had called me three days earlier to confirm that she would be at mine for two. When I saw the missed call, I texted her back to say that three was fine, but then she rang again, instead of replying to the text. She did this several times, until I thought that it must be a generational thing. I got up to make more tea and she followed me to the kettle. When she noticed I was wearing blue nail varnish, she reached out and touched one of my hands and said that she didn't like this 'modern trend that young women have now for nails, sharpened to within an inch of their lives', and then quietly, into a tissue, she added, 'Apparently, they're all into witchcraft now as well.'

When we sat back down with our mugs, I noticed that her face was really puffy. She must have cried just before arriving, maybe even on the doorstep. She looked like she was going to cry again, but then stopped herself. It's not my fault that I look so much like my mum. I pushed the bridge of my nose with my finger and she looked puzzled, so I explained: 'Sometimes, when I'm tired, I forget that I'm not wearing glasses, and I push my face instead, thinking that I'm pushing up my glasses. I imagine I can still feel them.'

Suddenly, with a fear in her eyes, she said, 'Who will look after you now she's gone?'

As she was leaving she said, 'I normally have natural yoghurt with cake.' And I thought, *What a joyless life.*

20

WELSH CAKES 2,
OR,
THIS PAGE IS ABOUT NANS

My Welsh nan was beautiful, kind and smelt of Nivea. She seemed to wear the same clothes in winter as in summer. She drank fourteen cups of tea a day. Her favourite cup lived next to the teapot on the old Welsh dresser and everyone knew not to touch it. Her grey hair was once long and dark – the only other woman in my family with hair as dark as mine: something I have attached a lot of significance to over the years.

She wiped hands, brushed hair and tied shoelaces over and over again. I can think of few people who have been so entirely on my side without agenda as she was. I only knew her as an elderly person, and find it hard to picture her young.

She had left Merthyr Tydfil and gone to work as a lady's maid for a family in one of the big towns. When the lady of the house died, she began to look after the widowed husband. They fell in love, and had one child: my father. A lifetime of cleaning and scrubbing meant she would often press a hand against her lower back, in pain, and swear quietly to herself.

One summer, when I came home from primary school, everything changed. She had been baking, but she never just made one cake, there would always be at least three. She was living with us by now. The box room downstairs had become her bedroom. The cakes were laid out on metal cooling racks. My eyes went big with excitement and hunger. I picked up a Welsh cake, but as I brought it closer to my face the sugar looked burnt. But it wasn't just sugar; it was dead ants too, crushed up and sprinkled on the cakes. Others were still alive. I dropped it on the floor, wanting to scream.

That's how I discovered that she wasn't well. She would spend more and more time lying down after that day.

One afternoon, she asked me to fetch her a glass of water. I was so busy playing that I forgot to get it. She died a few days later. I thought that I'd had something to do with her death, by not getting the water in time. I didn't tell anyone about this thought. I should have done, then maybe an adult could have alleviated some of my anxiety, but children's thoughts are often secretive.

The Nivea smell slowly faded from the little room, and then one day it was a storage room for things like big towels, and big coats.

I wonder if we are born with the ability to mourn or if it is something we must learn, and, if so, who teaches us? Perhaps mourning begins the moment a baby first realises that it is a separate being from its mother.

I read somewhere that we tend to feel all loss at once. I think this means that you can't feel one loss without feeling every loss you've ever had. It's all one feeling, one loss.

Everyone is just a different type of mourner standing in their own type of rain.

21

BIG PINK CAKE,
OR,
DISPATCHES FROM INSIDE GRIEF

I'm never bored, which is not to say I'm happy.
– Annie Baker, playwright

11 February 2019, 6:30 p.m.

My auto-reply stated: 'Due to a bereavement, I won't be checking my emails for a while.' It was Arial size 11, and I forgot to take my number out of the email signature. I got lots of texts beginning 'I know you're grieving, but . . .' My laptop was on an oak Victorian drop-leaf, with the two hinged 'leaves' – which could be folded out to accommodate extra people – supported on pivoted legs that looked like small gates. It was the nicest thing I had inherited from my parents. I had not yet needed to fully expand it.

This was the first time I had looked at my emails since Mum died. I was checking them out of boredom and guilt, not because I was concerned about my career. I couldn't imagine ever wanting to be funny again. I decided that wanting to be a performer meant that something had gone wrong in one's childhood.

The wording of the auto-reply wasn't accurate. 'Bereavement' (singular) was wrong. It should've said: 'Due to losing my best friend and parents, in quick succession, I want to be left criminally alone for years.' The restraint of 'Due to a bereavement, I won't be checking my emails for a while' didn't capture the matted hair, unwashed sheets and dishes, the long, long sleeps and empty fridge. I had spent the past two weeks in bed, unable to move, numbly staring at nothing on the ceiling. I used my phone to google what was wrong with me. I scored seven out of ten on an online questionnaire, 'Ten Signs That You Are Having A Breakdown', and then scored eight out of ten on 'Ten Things That Happen When You Go Into Shock'. Once people have stopped calling, when the final person has dropped off the same bunch of flowers from Sainsbury's, when the texts stop, and the internet is down, then, you face it all alone.

Earlier in the morning, having been awake again for most of the night, I heard the neighbour use their Nutribullet, then leave for work. As an expression of solidarity, I decided to get up and get a glass of water from the kitchen. Because I had spent all my time with my bed, the living room looked like the main photo on an Airbnb listing. The only sign of life was a depression on the sofa from my body, and crumbs on a plate from an oatcake two days ago. My commute to work was shuffling ten paces back to bed in my dead mum's slippers, where it's back-to-back grief for the rest of the day.

I felt a pang of guilt at how privileged I was to be able to afford to grieve for this long. My friend, who works in an office, was told by her boss that time off for grieving was 'at his discretion'. She asked him if she could have a week, and his response was that he had 'been on the gov.uk website' and it said 'one or two days should be enough'.

I turned on the tap but no water came out. I vaguely recalled a text about some problem in my area with the water supply and that the repairs would be carried out during 'working hours'. The milk had gone off two days before, but I didn't remove it from the fridge – that was a job for someone stronger. I cut out two small cubes of apple, and pushed half a sleeping tablet into each one and swallowed them. As a child, this was how I'd watched Mum administer worm tablets to the dog. Once the drugs kicked in, I fell asleep and dreamt of water.

And now I was sat at the Victorian drop-leaf, still dozy, in front of the laptop, having slept all day. I was trying to engage with the outside world, or at least engage with behaviour that made it seem like I was engaging with the outside world. Emails wanted to know when I was going to feel better, and when they could expect a reply. All I wanted from those around me was more time. The thought of having time was the only thing that kept me calm. When I accidentally caught sight of myself in a mirror looking as pale as milk, I changed from my sleep outfit (pyjamas) to my depression outfit (elastic waist, baggy, black) to try to leave the house. I got to the spyhole in the door, saw two people laughing by a car and changed my mind, dressed up for no reason, telling myself I just needed another day. I was hoarding time. I felt a strong resistance to any demands or expectations, even small ones, which was the only way I knew how to control the acute anxiety. 'No' to the next few months left me with all I could cope with: the next second, the next minute, the next hour. I was protecting time. The dead had wanted more time too, more time to be alive.

I opened my laptop. There were two emails from the same sender, both marked 'Urgent'. What news could justify ploughing through my auto-reply? What dystopian vision of the world beyond my room lay within this urgent missive? I opened it, bracing myself for more bad news or bad admin. It was an email requesting me to be the voice of a crisp, in an advert for crisps. It was the perfect, low-risk test to see if I was ready to interact with people. Towards the end of the email, they had addressed me as 'Poppy' by mistake, which made the offer even more appealing: maybe it won't really be me doing the job after all? Maybe it will be this other person, 'Poppy'?

When someone dies, a huge terrifying ravine of experience opens up between the person before grief and the person after it. I hate the new person. I look back at the old person with envy: using fabric conditioner, slagging off her parents to her therapist and having no priority higher than trying to work out whether or not she fancies someone.

Instead, on this side of the ravine, I am the new person: so fragile that she cries if people raise their voice above a loud whisper, gets flooded with adrenaline every time there is a knock at the front door and feels cold even with a hot-water bottle. Death will do that to a person. The only relief on this side of the ravine is to recite the mantra, 'It's just grief. It won't kill me. I'll outlive it. It's OK.' I say variations of this several times a day. So I'll do anything for the chance to become someone else for a day. Let's hope this Poppy persona is more functional and extrovert than me, my Sasha Fierce. I agree to be the voice of the crisp.

There was bad news on arrival. Being the voice of a talking crisp meant a lot of 'creative collaboration' according to the advertising guys (a woman and two men called Tom). I was twenty minutes late because the entrance to the recording studio was an unmarked door between a comic shop and a block of flats. A large yellow ladder was leaning against the outside door. One of the Toms had to come out on to the pavement, and then move it, so I could get in. When I apologised for being late, he said, 'No sweat, we're here all day.' He gestured inside; on his thumb was a novelty child's plaster. Once inside, Tom ordered three Dr Pepper Zeros and showed me a short clip of the crisp in action. The crisp looked at things, scratched itself and jumped about: my job was to make the corresponding noises, such as *uh, ooh, mmm*. It had eyes but no mouth, so it was a challenge.

The sound booth was a small, airless pod containing a screen and a stool, which I could adjust. The guys sat in the adjoining room. They could see me through the big glass panel and I could see them. On the floor, in the corner of the pod, were four or five aeroplane-sized bottles of still water. I drank two. The antidepressants had given me a dry mouth and lips, and I didn't want the crisp sounding too dry or like it was on antidepressants: I distinctly remember Tom saying the crisp was 'happy-go-lucky'. I didn't want people to watch the crisp advert and think, 'Fuck, is that crisp OK?' The guys grinned impatiently at me through the glass when I opened the lid of the third bottle. I could only hear them when one of them turned a dial, but they could hear me all the time. One of the Toms rubbed his belly sleepily and mouthed something at me (he had forgotten the rule about the dial). I couldn't hear him, so I smiled apologetically and shrugged. The voice of the woman (who hadn't said her name, or anything else, yet) suddenly filled the pod: 'We're going to play you the first ad now, OK, are you ready?'

'Yes,' I replied with fake confidence. The first advert played and I stared and stared at the lively crisp, as if I were hypnotised, missing my cue to say *mmm, ooh or uh*. The ad stopped playing. 'Oh, I'm so sorry,' I said.

'No sweat, here it comes again,' she said, and she giggled into the mic, so I giggled back and said, 'OK, great, thanks. I'll try again.'

Suddenly, someone touched my hair. It was the hair at the crown of my head, where the fringe flopped over my left eye. The hand felt tender, but with square, meaty fingers. I felt the pads first push in at the hairline, comb down to the point parallel with the top of the ear, and pull away, letting the hair cascade back down. I turned round. No one was there.

My immediate thought was that there was a breeze in the tiny airless, sound-proofed pod. My next thought was something like, *Can sound waves move hair?* Finally, I concluded that it was head tension due to psychological stress, took a deep breath and said, 'OK, I'm ready.' There were three different versions of the crisp advert. Later in the week, the team would show the three ads to a room full of strangers and the strangers would decide which of the ads made them want to buy the crisps. I wouldn't be there when the strangers watched to explain to them what I was trying to convey with the sounds I was making, so I'd have to put every drop of expression into the small microphone a few inches from my mouth. Even though the crisp had no mouth, it did have eyebrows, which made the challenge a bit easier. They asked me to make the crisp funnier, but I'd already made it as funny as I could.

The more Tom, Tom and the anonymous woman tried to humanise the crisp, the less human I felt. In fact, their attempts to anthropomorphise the crisp were so lazy that it made it more human, in the sense that any object with no features, with no expression at all, makes it easier to invent feelings for it. Even rocks and huge faceless stones can sometimes feel like big parental souls looking down at me. I don't know if you've ever visited the famous standing stone at Goonhilly Earth Station, in Helston, but if you have, then you'll know what I'm talking about. In the same way that the monolith at the end of the bed in *2001: A Space Odyssey* feels like a presence.

I said my goodbyes to the Toms and the woman (anon), and took a business card from reception so I'd have something to read in the lift down. Once I was alone in the lift, I saw a notification on my phone that I hadn't filled out my feelings journal on the app that day. It was a self-care app. Every day, you chose from ten faces, on a scale from very happy to very sad, and elaborated by typing details into a hospital-green box below. On some days, it was easier to just click on a face, and leave the box blank, because language fell apart under the weight of despair. On other days, I would click on the neutral face in the middle, which the app interpreted as progress, but it was more like going from despair to blankness, which wasn't progress, just a different shade of depression with less energy. Even so, I looked forward to using the app every day and being informed whether I had gained or lost sadness points. Even on days I couldn't get out of bed, I still cared about the app's opinion. I liked the attention, the constant notifications and the tailored ads. I put my phone away and ripped off a small corner of the card, but totally unconsciously. I think I had a lot of unexpressed anger still, because of all the trauma. The app didn't measure anger.

As the lift reached the ground floor, it happened again. The same tremulous hand laced its fingers through my hair. I swivelled round, expecting to make eye contact with a person, the sensation was so strong, but there was no one there, just my reflection in the lift mirror. The doors opened and I stepped out.

20 February 2019, 3:30 p.m.

Dialogue from the follow-up appointment with the psychiatrist who prescribed me the antidepressants about a possible repeat prescription:

Psychiatrist: Have you made any plans?

Me: Holiday plans?

Psychiatrist: No, to kill yourself.

Me: Oh, no. No, I haven't.

Psychiatrist: Good. So, how have you been getting on with the medication?

Me: OK, but they've taken away my appetite.

Psychiatrist: Yes, I can see that.

Me: ?

Psychiatrist: How much weight have you lost?

Me: I don't know. I don't weigh myself any more.

Psychiatrist: Why not?

Me: Because it's bad for my mental health.

Psychiatrist: So, apart from the loss of appetite, what other negative side effects have you experienced?

Me: Being too bold.

Psychiatrist: How is that a negative thing?

Me: Well, now I'm on these meds, I have a glimpse of what life would be like without anxiety, and it's terrifying. I keep doing confident things and telling people my secrets and really letting people in, you know, to the point of embarrassment. I realise now that my inhibition was actually keeping me safe. All this new confidence prevents me from accurately assessing my true abilities: I think I'm great. I'm acting like someone who went to private school. I'm so confident on this drug that I don't feel safe. When, and it's a big when, I come off the drugs, I will cringe at some of the things I've done, which other people would think were normal, I'm sure. I feel like I'm being lied to by a really co-dependent group of friends who are lying to me because they don't want to lose my friendship.

Psychiatrist [*finishing his final nod*]: Can you give me an example of some of the confident things?

Me: I invited some people to my home who I didn't really know.

Psychiatrist: Right.

Me: I felt, like, really mystical on Thursday and went into Sainsbury's and couldn't believe how beautiful everyone looked.

Psychiatrist: I see.

Me: I gave my number to a Hollywood actor, a really famous, good-looking one.

Psychiatrist: OK. Is there anything wrong with doing that? Did they want you to give it them?

Me: Yes, I think it's obviously a cringe thing to do, but I'm too tired to talk about it today.

Psychiatrist: Tiredness is a sign of –

Me [*interrupting*]: I think he did want me to give him my number though, yes. This was two weeks ago, so obviously I was two weeks younger and hotter than I am today. It's a subtle difference, but I can see it.

Psychiatrist: Right, well, this sounds like healthy behaviour, I would say. Nothing wrong with –

Me: But what would we even talk about? I don't think he was even that bright. I just felt an attraction between us, but I was probably wrong, it was probably just the meds talking slash flirting.

Psychiatrist: OK, well, putting the actor to one side, I mean to be opening up to people, staying in connection, that's all good. It could be that it just feels scary and new. Are you familiar with the idea: *Known hells are preferable to strange heavens?*

Me: Yes, I know what that means and it's not that. I'd say if it was that. Nah. I'm being really intense with everyone and connecting too much. It's off-putting. People don't want to know all this.

Psychiatrist: Right, well, I think it's just about finding the middle ground, a balanced way to communicate.

Me: The other thing is that I feel like I'm cheating by being on these drugs, like I am just cheating my head into thinking it's better. I need to spend this time grieving, not feeling better.

Psychiatrist: I think you need to stay on the medication. So I'm going to prescribe another six months' worth.

Me: I can't write well when I'm on it.

Psychiatrist: It might be that the writing is just different.

Me: I don't want it to be different, I just want it to be better.

Psychiatrist: It might make the writing more positive in tone.

Me: But then it wouldn't be true or . . . interesting to read.

Psychiatrist: I would be interested to read it . . .

Me: ?

Psychiatrist: Are you sleeping?

Me: Loads.

Psychiatrist: Good.

Me: But during the day. Is that bad?

Psychiatrist: Well, I think that you are clinically depressed.

[*Beat*]

Me: Go on.

Psychiatrist: I've no doubt. I think that this anxious, negative voice is the depression talking, not you.

Me: Interesting. Interesting. Well, I think we are one and the same.

Psychiatrist: Do you think this is something you've always had?

Me: Yes, I think so. I've always been a melancholic . . . [*searches for the word*] person.

Psychiatrist: What do you enjoy?

Me: But I'm not bored easily, which is good.

Psychiatrist: As in, what do you enjoy?

Me: Well, I guess I'm interested in lots of stuff. That's why I'm always getting things in my eyes.

Psychiatrist: What do you mean?

M: Yeah, I'd say about twice a week I get something in my eye: dust, insects, bits of a branch or something. Because I'm curious, you know: walking around with big eyes all the time, taking it all in.

Psychiatrist: Mmm. Have you heard the term *dysthymia*?

Me: Not sure.

Psychiatrist: Well, it's a long-term, low-level depression.

Me: What does it mean?

Psychiatrist: Well, it's a mood disorder, in that it can be a persistent mild-to-moderate depression. The word means 'ill humour'.

Me: That's funny.

Psychiatrist [*not smiling*]: Yes. So, I'm going to prescribe another six months. Try and do some nice things for yourself, hobbies you enjoy, that kind of thing. Last time we spoke, you said you used to go to life-drawing classes, that kind of thing?

Me: Yep.

Psychiatrist: Do you have any pets?

Me: Um, I have a plant and, um, a very high-maintenance printer – I don't know if that counts. . .

Psychiatrist: Right, no. And is there anything else you want to ask me?

Me: Aren't I just in mourning? Isn't that different from depression? Have I really tried all other methods to help myself before I take these? I don't want to just be . . . a happy machine, with no soul.

Psychiatrist: The grieving certainly will get easier, but I think that you need that bit more support, and the drugs will give you that. Think of the meds as extra friends.

Me [*holding one of the foil pill packets in my hand*]: Do you know that, I think it's a poem – something about how each pill is lonely and separated from its neighbour, like they're all in pill prison?

Psychiatrist [*putting his glasses away in the drawer*]: Yes, very poetic.

Me: Aw, thank you.

[*Beat*]

Psychiatrist: Keep connecting with people, hmm?

21 March 2019

One month later, Me books a life-drawing class.

I'd done the best dick in the room and everyone knew it. This was despite being the worst painter in my life-drawing class. It was a beginners' course, but the standard was unusually high. At least seven out of the twelve people on the course could have gone all the way to an intermediate or even *advanced* life-drawing class. I wanted to know what makes a person with such a level of skill choose a beginners' course. Was it out of modesty? Was it the desire to be the best artist amongst the dilettantes? I didn't think it was my place to ask every single person on the course what their motivation was. But I did tell a woman called Kathy, 'Wow, you are so good at necks, you should be in intermediate or advanced.' She smiled and nodded and said, 'Well, I can't do Wednesdays and intermediate is on Wednesdays.' Her motives had been less about status and more practical than I'd considered, so I decided to give everyone the benefit of the doubt and dropped my hypothesis. Whatever their reasons, I was there, at the behest of the psychiatrist, to see if art could save me. Creating is an act of hope and optimism. The art class was something new, and it was good to do that because every day can start to feel and look the same when you are grieving.

The high level of talent in the class was the reason I was particularly thrilled with my immense dick, painted in week six. The teacher, who I wanted to impress, made jokes a lot, but was deadly serious when it came to our work. She stood by my easel, commented on the good proportions of the head to the torso, pointed her pen at the dick area, and said, 'A lot of expression with detailed brush marks, well done.' I stood and admired it after she left. She was right, it was very expressive and this is because the secret to drawing a good dick is to study it as if it were a face.

The teacher had warned us that from week six onwards we couldn't just stuff our paintings into our folders at the end of the class and go: we had to display them on the wall behind us, using the White Tack provided. My psychiatrist had stressed in his email that I should just do 'forms of creativity that weren't going to be judged, only for therapeutic value'. But now the twelve of us were promenading around the small art studio, including Yani (the life-drawing model, now in a dressing gown) examining each other's efforts. The others looked at my dick with real envy, surprise even. The contrast between the finely detailed dick and the loose, broader brushstrokes used for the rest of the body led the eye straight to the groin. When Yani saw the painting he nodded at it and smiled at me from across the room. I smiled back a bit uncomfortably and wondered if my people-pleasing had kicked in yet again: does it affect how you draw someone's dick, knowing that the owner will see it?

We had been painting Yani's body in different poses for three weeks. I would place my easel at different points in the room, to vary my vantage point, but every time I looked up, to start work, I would be looking at his bum. I started to take it personally that Yani wasn't showing his front to me, but I knew that this was ridiculous, but that's how the voice of depression speaks. I had no choice but to become good at drawing bums. In week four I painted Yani's bum using only two colours: ultramarine blue and cardamom yellow. It was a very energetic image.

That morning, my app's *Positivity Reminder* had been *Everything you need, you already have.* I had immediately gone into Settings to see how you turn them off. But now, looking at Yani's bi-coloured bum, it all made sense. I didn't reach for more paint. I already had enough colours. That night, I turned the *Positivity Reminders* back on. Over the coming weeks, aphorisms included *What would you do if you knew you couldn't fail?* (wear white more often) and *Treat others as you would want to be treated* (wear deodorant).

When, in week six, I placed my easel by the window and looked up, expecting more bum, I was a little surprised to see Yani's dick hanging down like a massive finger. I think that's the other reason I had painted it so successfully: the shock of the new.

Later, as I was pulling my painting off the wall and picking at the White Tack with my nails, Yani came up behind me and said, 'Can I have it?' If I ever run out of money, I'll remember to pay my psychiatrist in dick paintings.

Sometimes I'd lie in bed and my body would say, 'No, thank you,' to everything, even some gentle art. That's why I was late for class in week seven. I wanted to sleep instead. Sometimes cancelling is the right thing to do when you are depressed, and other times I would feel better for forcing myself to leave the house and blend in with the non-mourners. Experts say not to make any big life decisions when you are mourning the death of a loved one. They don't mention that small decisions are equally hellish. I forced my body to go to the week seven class because it was our final lesson.

When I arrived, the class had already begun. There was a new life model: a man in his twenties with shoulder-length dark hair, parted in the middle and tied back. From my corner of the art studio, nearest the big windows, I was looking at his side. His left arm was bent, resting his hand on his hip, behind him, his head tilted to one side and he was smiling slightly. When the fun teacher saw my first sketch she asked, 'Are the toes on the right foot really directly beneath the forehead?' She was right, they weren't. I wasn't really looking. I was too distracted by my own inner critic. I recalled the psychiatrist saying something like, 'Try not to analyse what you're doing, just create for relaxation.'

On the wall behind the life model was an anatomy diagram showing a skinless male body. The muscles around the mouth looked like a secondary larger, toothless mouth. In week one, the teacher had shown us a 3D animated tutorial on YouTube of joints in motion. I had to look away from the ankle joint teetering and flexing: I wasn't ready to engage with human anatomy yet, it was too morbid. If I was at home, and wanted to practise drawing, in the week, I would have to look in a mirror, to think about anatomy and proportion. I would start to think about my internal machinery and feel on edge.

Instead, my shoulders now dropped with the relief of focusing on someone else's body. I watched my hands moving across the paper and had the odd feeling that they weren't my hands. They looked like the hands of someone who had been through something, and totally separate from me. But they must be mine, because they looked so much like my mother's hands – delicate, refined with long fingers – and nothing like the hand that had touched my hair, which was more like my father's. I was capturing life to help process death. When I spotted the dark blue-green bruise above his left hip, I was reminded that the vulnerability of bodies is never that far away, and I could have cried easily, if someone had made me jump. I included the bruise, and when I stood back to admire my painting on the wall, like the dick the week before, the bruise was the first thing you saw.

The popular teacher had brought in some wine and paper cups, and a retired lecturer in a kimono had made a large chocolate cake, wrapped in three layers of tin foil. Though we had only known each other for seven evenings, I would never see them again, so I was relaxed. If someone had passed by and peered in, we would have looked like a group of teachers relaxing at a grammar conference. As the art instructor made a little speech at the end, thanking and encouraging everyone to keep practising, Kathy (the best painter) and I sat on the long wooden worktop, which made it feel like we were hanging out in a sauna. 'Will you carry on painting?' I asked. 'No, I'm moving to Shrewsbury,' she mused. When the wine was passed out, I tidied up instead. In the deep stainless-steel sink, I placed all the plastic paint palettes, large brushes and jam jars full of tinged water. I was terrified to drink alcohol. I hadn't drunk since my best friend or parents had died. I was scared that if I drank, then the final bit of me would forget that hating myself was not what I deserved.

Kathy, also anti-wine, helped me to pull all the masking tape from the wooden easels. I scrunched all the bits up into a small parcel. Then we both collapsed our easels back down, and stood holding them like sandwich boards. I gestured towards hers, to indicate that I could put hers away too, as I was closest to the cupboard, where they were stored. When she smiled at me and pressed the easel into my hands, our stomachs lightly touched, we were the exact same height, and for a brief moment I imagined a whole future with her in Shrewsbury, buying masking tape in bulk, online, for our small lean-to art studio and how happy and calm we were in the countryside.

I placed the small parcel of masking tape on the teacher's desk, because I couldn't immediately see a bin. The teacher looked up and said, 'Thanks, Poppy.'

30 March 2019

I needed drugs to step outside the house and drugs to help me sleep. If there was an unexpected knock at the door or the neighbour made a loud noise with one of their new kitchen gadgets, I would jump like a shih-tzu that's been rescued from a quarry. Several brown packages were missed.

One afternoon, I wondered if the constant headaches might be lack of oxygen from being inside too much, so I placed a chair next to the open kitchen window and sat for a few moments with my head poking out, like a guppy coming up for air from its murky tank. Just below, I heard the neighbours discussing me.

'I haven't seen her for ages.'

'No, nor me.'

'Last time I saw her, she was going to a funeral, so . . .'

'I bet it's something to do with that, then. Oh, I don't like funerals.'

Overhearing myself being talked about was unsettling, like hiding as you watch someone look for you. I tried to make no noise and breathe shallow breaths in through the window, just above their heads.

The postman helpfully began leaving packages leant up against the front door. The packages contained things like depression memoirs, earplugs, hairbands and bubble bath for kids (kinder to skin). I was stockpiling, preparing for more weeks of grief. I couldn't stop the emotions, but I could prepare for their arrival. There were nights I wasn't smart enough to work out if time would make it more or less difficult to live without the people I loved. There were nights I would scare myself with the thought of future pain. In the day, I tried to distract myself with pain that was more manageable and familiar: men, work failures, politics, reality TV, other people's mistakes, etc. At one point, I even painted a table grey and read a book on the history of mazes.

*   *   *

When it comes to grief, we've probably all read the same books and articles and tweets: we all understand the concept of self-care and what we should be doing to help ourselves. Knowing self-care and wanting to do it are two different things. I began to notice wounded women everywhere I looked, and in the obvious places, like in books and on Facebook. I'd see myself in the women on reality TV (I would recognise which ones had suffered the most offscreen, then google them and would always be right). And when I was forced to go outside to do the recycling, I watched the woman who leant on the railings on the street opposite handing out small white cards. The app told me to meditate. But how, when you want to flee from yourself? I closed my eyes and realised that there was no saviour there in the silence, in fact it was the worst place to be. Any meditation was simply a meditation on pain. I clicked the face left of the middle, the least unhappy.

After watching the Marie Kondo programme about tidying, I decided to move the bed to the other side of my room because the neighbour who loved gadgets had now started banging doors. I thought the wall on the other side would be a fresh start. But that night, coming through the new wall, I heard a man groan, then shout one or two words, then silence, then the same thing another four times. It began to wake me up and did so on the next four nights. On the fifth night, I tried to record the sound on my phone, but when I played it back in the morning, it sounded like nothing. The following night, I was still awake at three in the morning, when I heard him cry out in pain. With a glass against the wall I heard new sounds too: he was watching a repeat of *Coronation Street* and he was repeatedly saying the word, 'Ow,' quite calmly, every five seconds or so. I could feel his distress pass through the wall and into my body. I put earplugs in and read a small section of *The Odyssey*, until my mood had calmed.

When I stood in the kitchen one night, and realised that my dressing gown was covered in dried soy sauce, I wondered how long it had been there and why I didn't remember eating soy sauce. The new dressing gown I subsequently ordered got sent to a flat in the block next to mine. This meant leaving through the main door and going outside. I put on loose jeans and a coat over my pyjama top, doing up the coat buttons all the way to the top. I hadn't showered, but I sprayed body spray into the air above my head and stepped forward into the mist.

I was living in a flat in one of three imposing Victorian buildings which had all been converted, situated along a busy main road. My interactions with my neighbours were minimal but polite. We weren't much of a community and people often moved in and out. Growing up in a small village, you weren't anyone until you were the subject of gossip at the telegraph pole in front of the Post Office.

One of the permanent features was the small group of drug dealers. At first, I was intimidated by having to walk through them, as I am by walking through all groups of conversing men. But no one would break in whilst they were there, so I started to view them as security and made peace with their presence. Once they saw my face enough times, they were friendly. The oldest one always asked me what was in my shopping bags and what I was having for tea, and I always told him.

Though I was tired, my mind was still busy and anxious as I stepped out on to the main street. There were several noises at once: a bus engine roaring, a siren and a homeless man shouting at a learner driver. It was only a short walk to the neighbouring block, but avoiding bodies on the pavement took the same level of concentration and skill as threading a needle. This was the particular way that the grief was manifesting itself that day, as an overwhelming sensitivity to the physical world. My whole body was like one big feeling. The main door had a buzzer system, but it was already open. I went inside and up three flights of stairs to flat number six and rang the bell. It occurred to me that the flat opposite this one, number five, was where the night-time cries must be coming from. Several letters and a flyer for a pizza place were sticking out of the letter box. I heard someone approach the door in number six, so I spun back round, helpfully holding the 'Sorry we missed you' delivery card level with my chest, like a high score for a gymnast, to indicate I wasn't a threat. A young girl of about ten wearing a very large purple backpack answered the door. The backpack was bigger than her whole torso. She seemed unsure if she should talk to a stranger, so she looked at my feet rather than my face, until a woman came to the door smiling and handed me the package. I took it with both hands and thanked her. The girl stood behind her mum, but now holding a Teletubby doll down by her side. I remembered standing behind my mum. When I suddenly enquired if the woman knew the person who lived opposite, her smile turned into brief suspicion then defensiveness. She leant on the door frame, blocking my view of the little girl, lowered her eyes and took in a deep breath through her mouth: 'He's not there at the moment.'

'I just wondered if he was OK. I heard him through the wall and I wasn't sure if he needed help or . . .'

'Yeah, he has people who come round and help him, so you'd have to ask them. He's a lovely bloke, John.'

'Yeah, no, I'm sure. I just hoped he was OK.'

'Well, he's only here for a few weeks at a time because he goes to a halfway house. I'll tell him about the noise.'

'No, there's no need. I'm fine. It's fine. I just hoped he was all right.'

'I keep an eye on him. We all do.'

'Thanks again, for the parcel.'

'OK, no worries. Bye then.'

She closed the door and I was left with my own thoughts, namely, *Oh my God, what's her problem – I was being a good person.*

When I got back to my building, the older dealer was there. 'Haven't seen you in a while?' he said. 'Oh, I've been working,' I lied and quickly went inside. I noticed a letter in my letter box, from the police. There was a special number to call if we saw anyone selling drugs and were concerned. I put the letter on the pile of unopened letters. The sleeves were too short on the dressing gown, and it was a different colour to the one I wanted. I kept it on anyway.

I don't know what I did with my time during this period

of bleakness. Reading was too difficult, TV hurt my eyes. My voice sounded croaky when I would engage in conversation. Some people adapt to change quickly. I'm not one of those people. Sometimes my thinking would involve daydreaming about the dead as if they were still alive, and I would have to stop, go back and change the person from present tense to past tense. It was as if I were taking every single memory I had of that person and moving them on a desktop from a folder called 'Alive' to one called 'Dead'. The process was exhausting and extensive. One afternoon, I awoke and couldn't remember what D's mouth looked like. How could I have forgotten so quickly? I don't want to forget, ever. The dead are fading in my mind. I cut out photos of my parents and glue them inside my grandmother's locket. They resemble two Elizabethan miniature portraits – often painted when a family member or loved one was likely to be absent for some time. The locket is too impractical to wear/ doesn't go with anything, so I hang it by the door instead.

Threes were difficult. One on one was easier. When two friends came round, they spoke too loudly, then started a conversation with each other and I felt left out of my own help. Whilst they talk about work, I open the self-care app. It asks me if I have eaten sugar today. Wait, does it want me to or is it saying I shouldn't? Someone on the sofa opposite says, 'I just feel like Angela's pushing me out.' People brought me a lot of cake and it became a burden. It weighed on me. When a cake appeared I would think, *All of this will get eaten, or all of this will get thrown away. There is no middle.* A neutral reaction to the cake wasn't possible. I felt stretched between two places at once: friends, work and facial expressions in the world of the living, and me, alone, with my memories and private pain, in the world of the dead. It was hard to be a good friend: I was too full of my own pain.

And that's when I thought that I needed to be with other mourners.

10 April 2019, evening

I had stood on my own outside the building until nine minutes past, wondering if I had got the day wrong. Grief support was on a Tuesday night. I pulled out my phone to check it was Tuesday. It was. Everyone else had just been late, probably too busy at home, grieving. Nine or ten people eventually showed up. As we shuffled in, I chewed my nails, they were only a few more chews away from needing plasters. Someone was putting out plastic chairs in a small circle. I wasn't sure how grief would fit into a physical space like this church basement. If grief could be measured, it would be on a scale exponentially bigger than that used for rooms, furniture and even intergalactic distances. But I kept showing up. I had to go somewhere and it may as well be there.

'How is everyone doing?' the therapist would say at the start of each session, with genuine concern. He was a guy in his forties, with a shaved head and covered in tattoos that had faded to light green. Every time he said something wise, I was embarrassed to have faked my initial niceness towards him. I didn't sit next to him at first. I had completely misjudged him based on his fierce exterior and now I was ashamed of myself every time he spoke with such gentleness. This new therapist didn't look like a therapist and other people's grief didn't look like my grief. I was even having to grieve my old ideas.

The basement room had no view, which felt right for a cross-section of mourners. We dimmed the lights and told stories about ourselves to each other. Then, after I'd returned home, I would repeat parts of the stories back to myself, reciting them like soothing bedtime stories.

I had to suspend my disbelief to think that one day there might be more to life than just grief. But I couldn't do it. So the group suspended my disbelief for me, and all I needed to do was show up. The group was helping.

Trauma doesn't have to be a social drawback. I liked everyone there.

Over time, the room got bigger, and the grief got smaller.

19 April 2019

I had remembered my fondness for miniature things. It was an interest I hadn't thought about since childhood. I got so much pleasure from just looking at miniature things. Someone told me once that real artists can get all the joy they need from life just by looking. At home, I had a shelf with a small collection of shrunken objects, right next to the door, which included two miniature cakes on a miniature table and two tiny portraits of Jacobean women with dark hair.

There was a knock at the door, which made me jump. I climbed out of bed and quickly scanned the floor for any clothes that didn't look like bedwear. Finding nothing, I grabbed a long black dress and swiftly put it on over my head. When I opened the door, there was a delivery guy, shouting at me for not answering the door more quickly. He was halfway through filling out a 'Sorry we missed you' card and was about to post it through the letter box. I tried to explain, but he just got louder and bared his teeth more. 'Didn't you hear? Why didn't you answer the door? Didn't you hear?' he kept repeating. Suddenly I was yelling too, 'I'm DEPRESSED. IT'S NOT MY FAULT,' I sobbed and took the package, slamming the door on his sunlit face. I could still feel his anger through the door. I stood still, tightening my hands around the package, waiting to hear him move. He said something to himself and left. I returned to my bed and rewatched the whole exchange on my doorbell camera app. Inside the package was a miniature house that I didn't remember buying. It looked like my mum's house in Tenby, the one she had moved to after Dad died, but where she very quickly died too. The receipt was in my name. I must have bought it in the dead of night without thought. Peering inside the little house was like projecting your consciousness into a newly discovered room; a world within a world. It made me feel in control. A way of controlling death, of compressing time.

Grief is spilling out of this home, out of the windows and on to the streets. Nothing can contain it.

I wrapped up the remainder of a big pink cake that a friend brought round and left the flat. The gang of men aren't there. A few metres from the main door, the old woman who leans on the railings across the street approaches me with a well-meaning smile on her face. 'I have a message for you,' she advises me, then hands me one of her small white cards. Printed on one side it says: ' We need to talk' and printed on the other side it says: '– God'. I don't take it but I thank her and she smiles and touches my arm and I feel a little afraid of her. Walking away, I looked back and she was trying to hand it to someone else who didn't want it either. I thought of the time, years ago, when I was in a really awful play and bonded with one of the other actors. A few weeks after the show finished, we met for lunch. He picked the place. But it wasn't lunch, not really. His 'temple' was just next door, he said, and he suggested we go take a look at it first, before eating. I was too curious to say no. It was a normal-looking building, with about forty people inside, all chanting in another language. It was a lunchtime 'service'. The actor and I stood at the back as the rhythmic sounds reached a climax. A few people were now dancing in the side aisles. Everyone hugged but I passed. The people sat on cushions and gave testimonials about how being part of the group had changed their lives. There were a lot of out-of-work actors there. I was completely unmoved and sceptical, but clinically fascinated. It wasn't until they asked if there was 'anyone new' that I needed to get out. I pretended to go to the toilet and then left and went home. On the bus,

I googled the name of the group. It had cult status in some European countries, but not all.

God might have wanted to talk to me, but I didn't want to talk to Her. Feeling this vulnerable, when my defences are down, I can't be trusted to protect myself. I'm 'Poppy' now and Poppy is always just minutes away from joining a cult (and then being a talking head in a ten-part Netflix documentary about the cult in twenty years' time after its dramatic end).

The buzzer was still broken on the door to the adjoining block of flats. The stairwell smelt slightly of piss and cigarettes. I held on to the banister like it was a walking stick. I heard the soft voice of the young girl with the Teletubby, which quickly stopped when she heard my feet on the stairs. When I saw the little girl playing in the stairwell, I could tell that her conversation with the Teletubby was supposed to have been private, because she looked flushed and was pressing her lips together in anger. 'Hello. Sorry,' I said. She tossed the Teletubby away from her, so that it fell down three steps. I picked it up and gave it back to her. She held the doll up by its neck and asked me if I knew what it was. 'Yes, it's a Teletubby,' I say. 'Are they babies?' she says, looking unsure. 'Well, I suppose they are cyborg babies, because they have televisions in their stomachs.' She begins to twirl about in the stairwell. Her mum comes out of the door to their flat and is a bit startled to see me. I indicate the object wrapped in kitchen foil, in my hands.

'I've had lots of cake, well, people have been bringing me cake, recently. I'm not going to eat it all, would you like any?'

'Oh, that's nice of you. Was it your birthday?'

'Yes,' I lie. 'Does John eat cake . . . I can, I mean it's for anyone really who would like some . . .'

'Oh, no. Sadly, he passed away,' she says very softly.

20 April 2019, all day

The new therapist asks me about my sleep patterns.

I hate going to bed. As soon as I go to bed, it means the day is over and a new day is coming. I hate the start of a new day because I've always suffered with morning melancholia. By evening, I've managed to get some personality. Every morning I start empty and have to begin the process over again. The second reason I hate going to bed is because night-time is my time. No one can get me or email me or expect things of me. I deserve that time and I want more of it, so I stay up later and later.

The next reason is that the night is a magical time full of fantasy and possibility, when I can make future plans: piano lessons, Pilates, metalwork. My best self seems possible at night. Then comes the horrible crashing sobriety of the daylight and all my desires feel stupid and silly. Suddenly life has lost all its mystery and profundity and feels nothing more than tiny incidental moments of mundanity: putting things in bins, yawning and emailing.

I feel closer to the dead at night, when my imagination is at its peak.

My therapist becomes very interested in this and asks me

if I ever remember a time when I was shamed for sleeping too much, so I tell her this story:

I've always slept a lot and I'm a good napper too. I once slept in the carpeted footwell of a truck, crossing Tanzania. As a sleeper, I would rate myself as probably the best in Europe.

In the summer before I got my A-level results, my mum was away a lot. I think she must have been working. My semi-retired father didn't cope well when my mum was absent. That's when I first remember being nocturnal, staying up later and later and then needing to sleep later and later, because teenagers still need a lot of sleep. But in the morning Dad would come into my room to wake me, and I would tell him I was awake but fall back asleep, and this went on all morning, with him getting more and more irritated. It was easier to just force myself to get up. I would sit at the kitchen table with him. He would then ask if I wanted a coffee. I've never drunk coffee, so I was always confused as to why he asked me every time if I wanted coffee. Actually, confusion isn't quite the right word, it was more like loneliness. It's the same feeling as when someone who knows you really well buys you a gift that you hate. Once Dad was occupied – watching Columbo with two slices of white buttered bread or mould-proofing the kitchen with moisture-resistant paint – I would go back upstairs and grab the duvet and one pillow from my bed. Locking the bathroom door, I would turn on the cold tap for a bit, to give the impression of bathroom activity, then turn it off. Bathrooms will always be a sanctuary for the sensitive. I treated the bathroom like a businessman treats his office – it was where I went to think and to nap and to be myself without interruption. I even left secret possessions in there: a copy of Elizabeth Wurtzel's *Prozac Nation* and a CD with a black-and-white 'parental advisory explicit lyrics' sticker on the front. I stored them on the bottom shelf of the airing cupboard, under the old curtain that Mum draped around Dad's shoulders when she cut his hair.

The textured wallpaper was of sprouting plants, with their Latin names written underneath in simple calligraphy, no doubt chosen by my mum for its classiness. The word 'erectus' was repeated a lot, to the point where it was oppressive. I'd make a small uncomfortable bed on the wood-effect linoleum, with my head near to the carelessly painted white skirting board. I'd lie down and read until I would drift into a sort of half-sleep, until Dad would knock on the door and ask what I was doing in there, about forty-five minutes later. I would leap up, stuff the bedding into the large middle shelf of the airing cupboard, splash water on my face before opening the door and saying, 'Just washing.' In the few moments, on the temporary bed, before drifting off into sleep, I would wonder, *If I spent the rest of my life in a locked bathroom, reading about other people's lives . . . that wouldn't be a bad life in many ways.*

When I get to the end of my story, the psychotherapist says, 'I think you slept a lot because you were depressed.'

1 May 2019

Today in grief group we were asked to bring in an object that best represented the dead person that we missed. I bring in a skull candle which reminds me of my best friend. A man brings in his partner's ashtray and a woman brings in her son's PlayStation.

'The last thing you forget is how they sounded,' someone says.

7 May 2019

I was in a dermatologist's office. She was feeling my head and asking me what I did and how my general health was and how long I'd had the touching sensation. I told her everything. 'Oh, comedy! That's interesting,' she said. A man briefly appeared in the corner of the room – her colleague, I assumed.

'You should write a comedy about dermatologists! The things we see!'

She laughed and turned to look at her colleague, and he laughed too and put something on her desk and left. She said she wasn't sure what the stroking sensation was, but not to wear my hair up every day or wash it every day, to 'give my scalp a holiday'.

9 May 2019

The neighbour is increasingly into gadgets. I saw her through the window last bank holiday, carrying a Bluetooth speaker in her hand. I've only been in her house once, last Christmas, for drinks and nibbles. She had a breadmaker and an electric whisk out on the kitchen work surface. The tree was up but undecorated. After an hour, I wanted to leave but her Brazilian partner said that I should help them decorate the tree, which felt too intimate, but I agreed because I was instantly tipsy after one beer. When her partner appeared with a ladder, to get the decorations from the loft, the gadget woman exclaimed, 'Don't you dare fall and die. I need you.'

Late May 2019

Sometimes, when we were smiling and chatting, it was easy to forget why we were there at the grief group. Even though the pain was always present on those Tuesday nights, it wasn't always immediately visible.

In my experience, when a person dies who gave your life structure and meaning, there are two forms of denial to choose from: pretend they are still alive, or pretend they never existed. There were whole sub-sections in the self-help area, dedicated to the subject of grieving, how to, how not to, and how to help someone else who has just lost someone.

I ignored most of it, because the emphasis on self-support and self-care was counterintuitive to me. I needed people, I didn't want to be an individual and I couldn't support myself or care about myself, not yet anyway. I had wanted to see mourning in the flesh, close up. The books also spoke of the stages of grief, as if it were a linear journey, but after my dear friend's death I became steadily worse over time, not better. The books just said 'seek medical advice' if you get worse. I craved vulnerability. I craved being around weeping strangers. More than that, the group meant I was accountable. Nobody wants to go through the grieving process. We want to revolt. Our small weekly meeting allowed me to honour the transformation.

A sniffing woman sat opposite me one evening. I had noticed her at my very first meeting. Each week, her clothes seemed to get more colourful and garish, as if she were trying to trick herself into joy. She was complaining about how loud the door buzzer was and how disruptive it was when it went off, signalling a latecomer was trying to get into the building. She had suggested banning latecomers because 'her nerves couldn't take the sound of the buzzer'. Everyone agreed that it was better to turn up late than not at all, and that lateness was even to be expected, given what people were dealing with. Everyone voted to allow latecomers in. She looked angry and smoothed her hair. 'Fine,' she said, 'but I don't want to be the person who has to get up and let them in.' All decisions were made as a group. 'Well, we could choose someone else to do it?' the therapist said gently. 'I'll do it,' I said. And that was always my job – to let people in.

The conversation that night was around how life had changed. People said they missed how a person smelt, or phone calls with them and private jokes. The sniffing woman said, 'I only eat fruit now. You can't survive on fruit, there's no protein in it. I do buy other foods, but I just look at them, watch them rot. I miss cooking full meals.'

She had brought in a home-made Madeira cake. At the end of the meeting the two of us washed up the mugs. As we chatted, she told me that she and her husband had organised a bake sale, to help pay for her son's funeral expenses. Lots of people had bought cakes they didn't really want, and she felt very grateful and emotional about that. Suddenly, I feel a wave of guilt and the thought that maybe not all loss is equal. 'Are you coming next week?' I ask. 'Oh yes,' she replied. 'Me too,' I lied, because I knew that I had got all I needed from the group and the weird stroking sensation had stopped. She shoved the leftover Madeira cake into her bag for life and closed her eyes for a moment. She looked not exactly pleased, but mischievous somehow. She said, 'Why don't I put cyanide in the cake next time? Then we can all go together, put us all out of our misery, what d'you think? To be with them – that's where we long to go, isn't it?' I put my hand on her upper arm, as if to show that I wasn't disturbed by what she had said, just in case she had disturbed herself by saying it, even though she had meant it as a joke.

Even later May 2019

I've started swimming.

The neighbours are quiet. They must have split up because a Portuguese dictionary and a *Vicar of Dibley* box set have been left out in the rain, next to the recycling, for anyone to claim.

Something about the repetitive motion of the strokes in the water seems to soothe my thoughts. I can only do twenty lengths, but I emerge out of the water feeling free. A nicer life is slowly emerging too.

I got drunk for the first time and didn't cry, but I did touch my miniatures too hard when I got in and broke one.

I open the app and it says, 'How are you feeling today?' so I press the first smiling face to the right of the neutral face. The app says, 'Well done on all the progress you've made.'

AFTERCAKE

> I would rather have had you by my side than any one of these words.
>
> — *Maggie Nelson*

Finding the benefits in loss and choosing whether or not to believe them

Being positive can come across as really creepy if you're not careful, but I'm going to give it a go anyway.

It is six weeks after I have written the first draft of this book, and I have returned to the beach on Abersoch Bay in Wales, Mum's favourite place. I lay down my grey crew-neck jumper and take in the waves. After a few minutes, I realise that I am completely unmoved by the view and still thinking about the stressful train journey there. Perhaps this isn't going to be the healing experience I expected. The sand in my nose and throat feels coarse, like sugar. The pure air is a shock to my lungs. There is no one here, which makes me feel fearful and exposed, and which I read in the *Wall Street Journal* is due to the animal brain's impulse to hide from potential predators. When two schoolgirls appear eating Milky Ways, leaning on a beach hut, I relax a little. I make a small 'o' in the sand with my middle finger as if drawing a musical note. I see her sat on the end of my bed, reading aloud from a well-worn copy of *What Katy Did*. It was my favourite book when I was little, or maybe it was hers. Mum must have read it to me so many times as a child. Halfway through the story, Katy falls from a swing and spends the majority of the book paralysed, in a wheelchair, looking out of a window. The second half is largely an examination of female pain, which is daring for a children's book from 1872. Sat looking out at the sea, I recall that because Katy is confined to her room she decides to make herself and her bedroom as nice as possible, so that people will want to visit her. Much of this past year has been an attempt to make my interior a nicer place. *What Katy Did* is the book I am named after.

A large wave forms and crashes. The water dispersing on to the sand sounds like the very distant laughter of an arena-sized audience. Another wave forms. Two small waves swash up, followed by a larger one. The waves are travelling in units of twos and threes, or I'm imagining it.

I take off my fashionable glasses, expecting to cry, but I don't. The light rain, the wet air and the waves seem to block the tears, as if one more drop of water might throw the whole world out of balance. 'You will always suffer more than others,' Mum said to me once, 'because of the way you are ...' As a kid I was often criticised for being 'too sensitive'. And yet I was also told that this sensitivity was perhaps the source, or even the price, of my (encouraged) creativity. Curiously, no one ever said I was 'too creative'. I've always known that tenderness and robustness coexist. Here, then, is the first positive: the grieving process has allowed me to value my ability to feel. I am grateful for it. Denying it and numbing it through all the usual methods seemed to make life worse anyway.

I count ten waves in one minute. With each wave, I will force myself to name a benefit of loss, a year on.

Another wave forms:

OK, well . . . my upset stomach and headaches have gone now and one of the greatest pleasures in life is things being over.

Another wave forms:

I find myself wearing clothes that my mother would not have approved of, i.e. anything too tight or too short.

Another wave forms:

I have a greater understanding of why people do the things they do when they are in pain.

Another wave forms:

Grief has created a pause to do more thinking and reflecting. I'm probably a less fun person now, as a result, which isn't exactly a benefit, but as an angry drunk comedian once said to me, backstage at a festival, 'There's more to life than just comedy, you know?'

Another wave forms:

I get to say, 'Look, I've been through a lot.'

Another wave forms:

Am much less scared of abandonment (on paper).

Another wave forms:

I don't always have to be thinking about the dead now, without feeling guilty, so more free time to do what I want. It wasn't my death after all, it was theirs. I don't know if I will outlive the grief or if the grief will outlive me. I might not need to grieve forever, who can say. There will be people after me who will still be grieving these people. I don't have to do all of it.

Another wave forms:

I'm less passive in my dreams now, which is a great start, and I'm hoping to be able to carry that into reality, in the next few months. So I think the positive here is: more courage.

Another wave forms:

Don't need to justify buying a longer phone charger so that I can comfortably lie in bed playing *Cake Shop 2*.

Another wave forms:

Identity. I've accidentally become more set as a person, because I don't have time any more to think, *Oh I'm going to be more like my friend B from now on* or, *Michelle Obama is so principled, I'm going to copy her*. There isn't time. Trauma means reacting in the moment, as you are. You have to be horribly yourself. I suppose my English teacher was right about character being revealed through action.

Another wave forms:

Breathe in, breathe out.

Another wave forms:

Grieving is a ritual and, by grieving every day, these rituals have taken on a meaning of their own.

Another wave forms:

I'm not scared of having a breakdown because I have already had one.

Another wave forms:

I notice which people listen and which don't now. And when I do talk, I talk more freely and with less embarrassment. Often listening is enough without offering solutions or getting competitive about who has suffered the most.

Another wave forms:

At first, death rendered all art meaningless, but now creativity seems like an appropriate response to everything.

Another wave forms:

I move quicker.

Another wave forms:

It's OK for me to have a bad personality. No one will judge you for about a year, when you've lost loved ones. You could go to the summer wedding of a good friend, and keep your sunglasses on and only talk to a dog and then leave, and no one would say anything the next day, for example.

Another wave forms:

Grief is wise, so I can trust the process and that it is taking me somewhere. Without looking, I trust that there is healing going on behind my back, all the time. I don't need to see evidence every day that I will get better and end up in a better place, just as the wave crashing on the beach began its life thousands of kilometres away when the wind blew over the ocean. Grief is ancient and began long before I was born. Grief is older than me.

Another wave forms:

I finally got a painting in the Royal Academy Summer

Exhibition. It's a nude woman, seen from the back, painted in blue, yellow and pink. Dad never knew, but he would have been so overjoyed.

Another wave forms:

More awe and mystery. Grief is like nothing else. It created more room for the unusual.

Another wave forms:

I can email my therapist 'in the week' if I feel I need extra support.

Another wave forms:

I'm closer to the living.

Another wave forms:

I might be equipped to help someone else now.

Another wave forms:

Appreciation. After a death, for a while, you are less alive, but then, if you're lucky, you will become more alive.

I'm still in the same room as the mourning, but I've moved to a spot where there is a little more light and fresher air.

There's a particular type of jealousy I feel now, when I see parents and children together. I'm jealous of their imagined lives.

Appreciation can be the antidote to jealousy. A small thing like having a nice peach will suddenly seem huge.

Another wave forms:

More humility and the good kind of not knowing. I now feel ignorant in a way that is liberating. It is liberating to admit powerlessness over something. And I can share with others the shame of knowing that we're going to die and the shame of how powerless we are over death.

This makes me think of the 'divine darkness' that Maggie Nelson writes about in *Bluets*. *Divine darkness appears dark only because it is so dazzlingly bright.* I like that. Some nights were so dark that they were transcendent: *a darkness beyond light.*

Another wave forms:

I have nothing new to say about grieving, but I still felt I needed to write about all my losses, partly because I was consumed by them. Even when I wasn't trying to write about loss, it would show up in whatever I was writing anyway. There are many reasons to write about pain: to create meaning or understanding, to elicit response, revenge, duty, to cling to it, because someone you look up to told you to, to connect with and help others, to demand people listen to your story, to document, to honour, an obsession with telling truths, to try to self-heal, or without reason at all. They all seem like valid reasons to me and I can relate to all of them. Though I would swap all the words in this book for having everyone alive again.

Another wave forms:

I'm alive. Not everyone does survive: loss can be fatal, I've seen it for myself.

Another wave forms:

I have a 'legitimate' reason to be sad.

Another wave forms:

Sympathy and attention. Now in my late thirties, I worried that perhaps less sympathy would be on offer. Maybe I am just about old enough to lose close friends and parents, less a tragic event, more an affirmation of the essential order of all living things. But there was lots of sympathy on offer.

Another wave forms:

Being forced to ask for help and realising how good it feels to be helped and held.

Another wave forms:

The confidence that comes from having overcome.

Another wave forms:

Sometimes, at night, I suddenly become dizzy with the thought, *They're not coming back.* Losing your parents offers you a chance to re-parent yourself, as you wish. But you may, of course, want to absorb some of the deads' traits too.

Another wave forms:

The final benefit is that I've begun to accept the ordinariness of life: less romanticising, because apparently it's bad for you, even though it feels so good.

It's just triumphs and failures.

Another wave breaks:

'I can't go on, I'll go on.'*

---

* Samuel Beckett

ACKNOWLEDGEMENTS

Thanks, especially, to Richard Roper at Headline Books for his encouragement, editorial wisdom and kindness. A huge thanks to Gordon Wise, Lily Williams, Debi Allen and Jess Lax at Curtis Brown for making this book happen and for their hard work.

This book would not have been possible without Adam Drake's creative input and patience.

I'd also like to thank Alara Delfosse, Yeti Lambregts and Mark Handsley.

Thanks to the radio-maker Kaitlin Prest for making the series 'No' about her personal struggles to understand and communicate about sexual consent, which influenced me greatly.

Thank you to Susie Orbach, Geneen Roth and to the women writers whose work inspired me to believe that I could write a book.

I'm very grateful for the friendship, support and guidance of so many, especially Henry Petrides, Marianne Buckland, Anna Starkey, Jane Houston, Sophie Black, Fionnuala Kennedy. Thank you to my family and to HP.

AUTHOR'S NOTE

Lastly, this book is a poetic response to life events. It is how I remember them and how I experienced them emotionally. All names have been changed. Places, timelines and job titles have been altered to maintain anonymity, and in some cases two people have been combined as one, for the sake of storytelling. If you think you recognise yourself or others, then you're probably mistaken, as details have deliberately been changed to ensure certain people never recognise themselves. Certain moments have been exaggerated for comic effect.